D0561578

Visitations from the Afterlife

Visitations from the Afterlife

True Stories of Love and Healing

Lee Lawson

HarperSanFrancisco
A Division of HarperCollins*Publishers*

Grateful acknowledgment is made to Parallax Press for permission to quote from *Call Me by My True Names: The Collected Poems of Thich Nhat Hanh*, by Thich Nhat Hanh (1993).

Index of art: p. 1, *The River*, 1987; p. 15, *Dream Jar*, 1993; p. 21, *The Mother Tree*, 1996; p. 43, *The Beloved*, 1999; p. 61, *The Potter*, 1996; p. 75, *The Kite*, 1998; p. 89, *The Gift*, 1997; p. 103, *The Weaver*, 1998; p. 121, *Demeter and Persephone*, 1999; p. 137, *Face #2*, 1998; p. 153, *Song of Morning*, 1997; p. 169, *Song of Night*, 1993; p. 187, *Ancient Trees*, 1997; p. 199, *Totem*, 1993; p. 217, *My Mother's Garden*, 1993; p. 225, *Song of Night #2*, 1996; p. 229, *A Dream of Trees*, 1998. All artwork © Lee Lawson.

HarperCollins books may be purchased for educational, business, or sales promotional use. For information please write: Special Markets Department, HarperCollins Publishers, Inc., 10 East 53rd Street, New York, NY 10022.

HarperCollins Web site: http://www.harpercollins.com

HarperCollins®, ✦®, and HarperSanFrancisco™ are trademarks of HarperCollins Publishers, Inc.

FIRST EDITION

Library of Congress Cataloging-in-Publication Data
Visitations from the afterlife : true stories of love and healing / [compiled by] Lee Lawson. — 1st ed.
    p. cm.
    ISBN 0–06–251653–1 (cloth)
    ISBN 0–06–251654–X (paper)
    1. Future life. I. Lawson, Lee.
  BL535.V57   2000
  133.9'01'3—dc21

                                            00–026196

Designed by C. Linda Dingler

00 01 02 03 04 RRD(H) 10 9 8 7 6 5 4 3 2

To Martin, Lily, and Harry—
a circle of love around me.

Contents

The Psychological Phenomenon
of Aeternal Love

As a psychoanalyst entering her fourth decade of clinical practice, I remain interested in the phenomena of human beings'
perceptions when they experience a heightening of, a lowering of, or
an opening in the threshold of usual consciousness, thereby experiencing additional dimensions of consciousness—ones that do not
disturb the health of the psyche but seem instead to strongly
enhance and invigorate. In one aspect of my early inquiries, I
worked to deduce the common environmental and psychological
factors conducive to visionary states of consciousness—their potential benefits and perils, both. It was in those inquiries that I first
realized empirically that self-reported external and internal psychic
experiences of the populace were far more extensive, far more common, than classical psychology had ever catalogued.

Over subsequent years, there have been more and more psychological inquiries into the nature of the so-called non-rational
aspects of psyche, such as "sudden knowings," precognitive
insights, "near-death" adventures, and "appearances" by the
deceased to the living. J.B. Rhine, the Theosophists, John Lilly,
Raymond Moody, and many others stand out as inquirers from

other fields, such as transpersonal philosophy, religion, and science. The gathering of such reports is useful for several reasons: one, for furthering the mappings of our understandings of the astonishing and seeming unending abilities that exist within "normal" human nature; second, to give assurance to those who are "sensitive" to these kinds of experiences, that events such as theirs have been similarly experienced by many throughout history; and third, to expand understanding that such are not the stuff of madness, but of an expanded and meaningful consciousness—forms and expressions beyond ordinary reality that can augment our understandings of humanness.

This book is about visitations, that is, about departed souls appearing to living souls in a way that can be palpably heard, seen, or sensed. By a preponderance of years listening to the psychological stories of many patients' lives, I find that the phenomenon of visitations does not occur "only to the holy few," but that they seem an accessible possibility in every life regardless of the mundane aspects of family, work, or religiosity unsundered.

If there is a fuel that "causes" the visitation to coalesce, it is most oft reported to be that of love and/or meaning between the living and now the dead. Upon this ground of affinity and/or love rest several psychological aspects of "visitations." The following is by no means a complete listing of aspects, but some of the most salient. First of all, "appearance" accounts and experiences are events that seem to the ego highly unusual in that they often initially occur outside the ego's usual expectation of "normalcy." Although to the greater self such heightened experiences feel compatible and are often awe-inducing, to the ego they feel somewhat like a sudden shower of sparks from out of nowhere. That the startled or puzzled ego reacts thusly can be considered normal. That the greater self reacts with happiness and/or peace would be considered normal, too. If the phenomenon continues or expands, a more balanced amalgamation of both will be made eventually, with ego gradually submitting to soul's insights on these matters.

In the classical psychology the experience of an apparition was once called *participation mystique*. This is a sudden satori-like ability to pass through the usual psychological and censoring boundaries of the ego, and "to see anew." People often report fresh realizations of uncommon, other-worldly images or sensations that stay with them for long after.

From many anecdotal reports we may glean that such "appearances" to a living person by a soul who has died from this world often seem to carry with them a heightened clarity of purpose. Images, words, sensations, thoughts are reported to be conveyed by the deceased soul "they once knew." Further, the departed loved one is almost always reported to be one who "resonates" in some significant way—this may or may not have been realized before that soul's physical death. Further, the visitor conveys that they care for the living person. They often want to instruct them, inaugurate change in them, or desire to reassure them in some manner that is *significant to the one visited.*

Whether visitations occur by summoning up desire for such—for instance by the "descent" into prayer and/or pilgrimage (practices undertaken by millions for centuries)—or by the fact that the appearance "suddenly comes upon one," as in many visitation reports, the subsequent sudden and heightened recognition of spiritual force not only unfolds, but most often afterward becomes a watershed event for the visitee *for life.*

That people have their own understandings and derive information from these kinds of experiences is a time-honored development across all tribes, all groups, all eras. Yet, what these events and visitations are made of, and how they coalesce exactly, we do not know. There have been many speculations about "extra-psychic" experiences, including "death and return to life," and life-be-saved-by-angels. Some say such numinous experiences are the result of the imagination working overtime. Some say they derive from wishful thinking. Some, more scientifically oriented but reductive, say they are misfirings of the brain that then cause the optic nerves to produce images that are not "true" in reality. But, the older I become, the more I see that one of the easiest errors of human nature is to too quickly press for "final answers to infinite questions." In so doing we root ourselves only in the ego's narrow

Archimedian-limited ability—one in which we cannot stand far away enough from the phenomenon in order to gain the largest picture needed to interpret it accurately. I tend to feel as I do with many things now, that the many such situations belong under the category of aeternal "God's business." I am more concerned that each soul who perceives these mysterious experiences understands them as fruitfully as possible: as strengthenings, as the offerings of goodness, as reuniting the broken ends of whatever each soul feels has been temporarily lost.

The categories of psychic experience belong more to the *Magna Mater*, a greater mother-body of phenomena than to the little island of the human ego alone. We should not rush quickly into a *consensus audacium*, a rash agreement just to try to overwhelm and "solve" the aeternal, but rather move toward a *consilio et anima*, an ever-more wisening of the soul. If we were to place, as the ancient Buddhists, Christians, Muslims, people of the Heath, Celts, and Jews do, the idea of higher power, Great God, The Greatest Knowing, at the center of these experiences, we can glimpse a state akin to that which the Hindus call *nirvana*, that is the eradication of all clashing oppositions. Then we sense that "visitations" themselves not only present an event in time, but infuse the visitee with a completely different kind of consciousness than before, one that can be called both transpersonal and transformative. In analytical psychology such a fastening of one's human mind to The Great Mind is called individuation, the experience of the undivided Self. This *unus mundus*, united world view, as it has been called since medieval times, is the living nucleus of visitations. As von Franz writes in *C.G. Jung*, 1975 (translated by W.H. Kennedy), "The most essential and certainly the most impressive thing about synchronicity occurrences . . . is the fact that in them the duality of soul and matter seems to be eliminated. They are therefore an empirical indication of an ultimate unity of all existence . . ."

Thus, when my patients ask me, "Is this real? Is this all right?" this "leaking between worlds," I reply that if it uplifts, helps, heals, enlightens, gives richness and goodness into your life, by all means. These are the experiences of the diminishment of the negative duality that exists in many over-enculturated societies wherein all aspects of heaven and earth are seen as opposites rather than as a continuum. These are experiences that help to restore and repair a too narrow and/or broken worldview.

There is a little wood plaque on my wall here at my desk. It is my first diploma. We were allowed back then to choose a glyph that was then hand-lettered onto the parchment in a beautiful script. I chose this saying when I was in my late twenties. Often ideas we once cherished years ago are not necessarily able to match stride with us as we gather more years, more insight. But, now, even as an *abuelita*, grandmother, I find this glyph ever more resting in a perfect space in my bones. It is this:

The world is a magical place, filled with astonishing things, patiently waiting for our wits to grow sharper.

The author and summoner of this book, Lee Lawson, so gifted in painting, now as storyteller, brings to readers a rich palette of some of the most important kinds of stories. She is a rare woman who is gifted with the strong charisms of great active love for humanity, and an almost unbearable faithfulness to the visions of meaningful soul life in self and others. This book is her love letter across the worlds, the evidence of a sensitive spiritual life, one that presents the case for *amor aeternus*, eternal love and unbreakable kinship between souls.

With these heartfelt stories in this little gem of a book, so may it be for all.

CLARISSA PINKOLA ESTÉS, PH.D.
Diplomate Jungian Psychoanalyst
Director, La Sociedad de Guadalupe
Littleton, Colorado; 2000

Introduction

Brokenhearted and tearful over the recent death of my dearest friend, I was sitting all alone in my studio when another old friend, Harry, quietly sat down beside me to help soothe my aching heart.

I should tell you now that Harry has been dead for a number of years. Many times since his passing he has come to me with his love, caring, and guidance, and over the years I have come to think of him almost as a beloved uncle who watches over me and occasionally steps forward with comforting words and a helping hand.

Harry's energy encircled me tenderly as I poured out my grief and the inconsolable feelings of loss that filled my heart. Then he said to me, "Here is a gift. You can write a book on visitations that will be healing for you and for others who read it."

My first response was an emphatic denial. "But I'm a painter! What do you mean, I can write a book?"

Harry went on to show me an image of the finished book, inside and out, and as he did he explained why this was my book to write, why it is needed to be written at all, and why now.

Harry showed me that because I have had many visitations in my life, starting in early childhood and continuing until the present, it is a subject that is a part of me, a subject I can speak about from the heart in a simple and direct way. Neither research and analysis nor explanation, this book would be a love letter, a gift given to me that I may share with others.

My own visitations have given me firsthand experience of the multidimensional reality of our lives and the presence of a larger life within which our earthly lives are cradled. My journals are filled with visitation stories that I have collected over the years, told to me by people from all over the world—their own stories, those of their parents, grandparents, aunts and uncles, brothers and sisters, and friends. Every visitation story I have heard has inspired in me a passionate interest in the healing and transformation that come to all who are touched by this wonderful grace.

According to Harry, every reader may share in the blessing, even people who have not personally had a visitation experience, because the very reality of the occurrence reveals that there is an afterlife. It says that we live in the context of eternity, not as meaningless blips on the screen of random events. We need this existential healing because there has never been a time when we have felt more disconnected from our true nature. It is time that visitations come into the open and be acknowledged. Treasured private experiences since the beginning of time, visitations have always been profoundly healing to those directly touched by their power. Now, Harry tells me, it is time for the healing to be extended. This book is just one of many avenues through which this healing grace is coming into the world at this time.

Many wonderful first-person stories from around the world are gathered here, each from a person who spontaneously experienced the unmistakable and undeniable presence of someone no longer alive in our world, the presence of someone who, for a moment, returned from the afterlife. Every story brings a deeply healing message of love, connection, and the continuation of life. What could be greater than visiting once again with the ones you love and knowing, in every atom and cell of your being, that life continues?

This knowing, which comes to us so resoundingly during a visitation, changes everything in our lives. When we know that this human life is just one part of an eternal journey, a journey taken in the company of our beloved friends and family, every aspect of life is recast in the larger arena of eternity.

Visitations bring personal healing between the individuals involved, usually of some aspect of their relationship that is important and meaningful to each. It may be the need to say good-bye, or it may be a more complex message, such as one of forgiveness or reconciliation or guidance. There are as many reasons for an encounter as there are people.

Any visitation can bring a deeply needed spiritual, existential healing, a binding of the heart and soul as we experience, beyond words or thoughts, a true relationship with the larger dimension of life. The unity and boundless nature of life are affirmed when we discover that what we thought is the end is not; instead, life is eternal. We enter into a new covenant with life.

Visitations from the Afterlife is not an analysis of visitations, nor does it try to explain or validate them. This is not about proof. I don't presume to know how or why visitations happen. I know only that they do in fact happen and that when they do, a profound healing often takes place. If you embrace the experience, it will change you inside and out and will influence how you live and move in the world for the rest of your life.

A visitation from the afterlife is an extraordinary moment in which we experience a tiny inkling of the true nature of the vast and infinite life we live. Not just about something that will happen after we die and leave this world, a visitation has everything to do with how we live this precious life, here and now, while still embodied upon the earth. It gives us assurance that there is more life to come. This is the great message of love that is at the heart of every visitation.

When I was a child, whenever anyone asked me, "What if you had three wishes?" I always used all three of my wishes wishing that I could live forever (along with my dog). I know now that I could have used those wishes for something else, something that I didn't already have, like a horse of my own. I really would have loved having my own horse; I didn't know then that I was already in the midst of living forever.

I offer you the blessing that comes with this gift, which has been so lovingly given to me, a gift of grace that enriches and heals me in every way, an experience that is very close to my heart. It is a gift that is inextricably woven into the fabric of my personal, creative, and spiritual life day by day. I invite you to read *Visitations from the Afterlife* with an open heart. These wonderful stories can bring healing to your heart and soul. They come to you with the blessings of many.

Chapter 1

Love Letters
from the Infinite

MAKING THE INVISIBLE VISIBLE

M oving closer to me, they always begin in a whisper. "Somehow I know that you will understand. Something wonderful happened to me once, and I've never told anyone about it. Looking at your paintings, I am reminded of that time, I'm not quite sure why."

The person before me goes on to tell the extraordinary story of a reunion with a beloved one who returned from the afterlife, a single moment that changed their life forever.

Over the years I, too, have had several deeply moving visitations from the afterlife. In each instance the person returned to me briefly to give me a message. Though the particular messages have been filled with love and healing, I have always felt most blessed by the greater overarching message of every visitation: we are spiritual beings living in a spiritual universe. Life is a continuum. We do not die, and we will be together again with those whom we most love.

I have had a lifelong enchantment with the mysteries of incarnation—of spirit taking form, of becoming embodied. As a visionary artist, I find that most of my paintings in some way address this ancient and ongoing fascination. Infinite, unlimited spirit chooses to come into form, into containment and seeming limitation. The creativity that emerges out of this paradox is endlessly fascinating to me.

Over the years many people have told me their treasured visitation stories upon seeing my work. I believe that for many people my images take them once again into that archetypal, mythic realm in which their own encounter occurred. Not here, not there, but in a third place, a place in between. A timeless place of meeting.

Visitations are bridges between the seen and unseen worlds, moments of absolute knowing and experiencing ourselves as unlimited by the material world. They create a vantage point from which to envision ourselves as finite and infinite, a picture of ourselves that is normally hidden from view.

Art, too, in its ancient and essential form, is a bridge making the invisible visible; it crosses the apparent distance between essence and form. Sacred, archetypal art functions as a portal, a doorway that opens to us the nonphysical realms that underlie and create our lives. Art, then, is a visitation when it gives us a vision of our own intimate connection with the unseen order.

Visitations from the afterlife are often powerful, life-changing events that reorient life around a central, expanded, sacred point of reference. These moments create a compelling picture of life as timeless and unlimited but also as intricately connected to the rich tapestry of our daily lives.

I love the particularity of each visitation story. Every encounter is profoundly personal and rich with shared meaning for those involved. At the same time, every visitation story is universal and deeply affects all who hear it. Every story has blessed me. Every visitation account that I have ever heard has healed some part of my soul.

I have always thought of visitations as love letters from the Infinite.

GIFTS FROM THE INFINITE

In a single moment of time, you are infused with the sacredness of your own life and of all life. This vision of the soul as an intricately woven part of the larger whole often has the effect of making your time here on earth seem more precious than ever. It creates a deep reverence for the ordinary.

Every visitation from the afterlife is a gift that comes to us unannounced and unearned. This elusive grace comes to people from every walk of life, every bent of mind, to those who believe and to those who do not. Visitations come to scientists, engineers and doctors, and other left-brained, rational beings as often as they happen to artists, writers, gardeners, and all of the right-brained intuitives among us.

With absolutely no regard for your ideas, your theology, your history, your beliefs, or your expectations, visitation experiences bypass the intellect and go straight to the heart and soul. You behold your true relationship to the unseen order, which underlies all of creation.

THE TREASURED SECRET

It has been estimated that millions of people from every area of the globe have experienced a reunion with a loved one from the afterlife. Why, then, are these visitations usually kept secret, told to a very few trusted friends or to no one at all?

Perhaps it was different in ancient and earlier times, but in recent centuries revelations and mystical experiences have not been spoken of publicly out of fear that one will be called a lunatic, a heretic, or, worse, a witch. When handed down by church or community, these judgments often resulted in severe censure, punishment, or even death.

So the precious stories of visitations had to be passed down secretly, whispered from parent to child, from friend to friend, from heart to heart. Everyone knew of or had themselves experienced the miracle of a few golden moments of reunion. Care was always taken that these healing stories be told only to those who could be trusted, who would understand the precious gift that was being given to help soothe a grieving heart.

Though in modern times we have seen an end to witch trials and the persecution of heretics, there remains a reticence about telling our stories openly. In the first half of the twentieth century you would have been considered mentally ill or unstable if you claimed to have had a meeting with a spirit. More than one poor soul was placed under psychiatric treatment for that "delusion." At the very least, falling on unsympathetic ears, the story might be thought the product of grief, medication, or wishful thinking. Better not to mention it again—for your own good.

Recent decades have seen a change in this attitude. Many people, awakening to the spiritual reality of their lives, are openly and actively seeking expressions of its myriad dimensions. Now we may openly give voice to the joy of revelation. This ancient voice will find many receptive, hungry ears.

You should know, too, that there is another quite different and important reason for holding a visitation experience in secret, at least for a while. Most spiritual and mystical traditions teach that when one receives a revelation it must be taken into the heart, not spoken of but allowed to take root and grow. To become cellular. To ripen and mature.

As a seed, it must be placed in the warm darkness of the fertile earth where roots will emerge and reach down to anchor it into the ground. In time, a sprout will appear, next a shoot, and then a stalk, and in its season the plant will bear fruit. When the fruit of that divine moment ripens in you, you will know it. Then you may give of it freely.

INTO THE LIGHT OF DAY

An encounter from the afterlife bears many blessings and evocative gifts. Some are profoundly intimate and personal, rich with shared meaning. The very fact of the visitation itself, though, bears the greatest gift of all. Resoundingly, the medium is the message. It reveals to us that we exist in a larger frame of reference, one that encompasses other realms of expression in which we participate as multidimensional beings. It shows us we are souls.

In this century we have been taught that we are specks of dust in a random, meaningless universe. Never before has there been a time when our cosmology has taken us so completely out of relationship with the Divine and left us stranded in despair. We suffer deeply, as individuals and as a society, the wounds that have been inflicted by this shattering of life into mere parts.

A speck of dust is a container too tiny to hold infinite spirit. A body, also, is too small. Even a lifetime sandwiched between two blacknesses of nonexistence cannot contain infinite spirit. The soul needs nothing less and has nothing less than infinity in which to express and create itself. The soul knows itself as eternal and immortal. We are feeling the soul's longing to enter the life of the world, just as the soul is feeling our deep hunger for its sacred presence.

It may be possible for the mind to conceive of nonexistence (though I doubt it), but the heart and spirit cannot. They ache to know that our lives are meaningful, spiritual, and ongoing. The existence of science does not negate the reality of the spiritual universe, just as the reality of spirit does not negate science.

There is a global reawakening to the reality of the unseen order, which underlies and creates every nuance of our existence. We are mind. We are body. We are soul. We are many things at once, everything at once. We must be able to hold seeming paradox without the need to throw out this in order to be that. The vessel can contain it all.

By telling our stories, we can begin to bring our souls out of hiding and into the light of day. We can celebrate the reawakened knowledge of ourselves and our true nature as multidimensional, multisensory beings. When the invisible is made visible, if for only a moment, we are filled with joy in knowing that we are part of a larger life that is forever and endlessly unfolding, creating and recreating itself.

AND THE ROOM WAS FILLED WITH LIGHT

The many stories that follow speak eloquently of the variety of experiences that can occur during visitation encounters. A reunion is perceived by senses beyond the five ordinary, physical ones. We have many bodies: the physical body, the emotional body, the mental body, the etheric body, and the soul body. Each has its own sensory modes. The nonphysical senses may remain out of conscious awareness much of the time.

During a visitation from the afterlife, even the five ordinary senses are extraordinarily heightened, often making the experience seem hyperreal. "More real than real" is often how people describe their visitation experience. Imagine all of your senses with the voltage turned up from a hundred to a thousand, ten thousand. A visitation is a heightened state of awareness that can be said to be to ordinary consciousness what ordinary consciousness is to dreams. It is an experience of presence, power, and awakening.

A reunion can be both an internal and external experience, perceived by many sensory modes at the same time. Some people experience the encounter as an external event, seeing with the outer eyes, as in seeing a solid embodiment of the visitor or seeing a less-tangible but still-visible form. Others hear with the outer ears a voice spoken aloud or bells or music. Changes in the light occur, from a subtle "something mysterious and odd about the light" to the sense of "seeing a blazing sun before my eyes."

Many speak of experiencing vastly expanded, more-encompassing awareness at levels that are deeper than those of ordinary consciousness. You are, for that time, in a separate universe, no longer in your own world and not in the realm of the afterlife, either, but an entirely other place that has been created in the overlap. The two of you are standing on a bridge spanning the opposite banks of the same river.

A reunion can come with the gentleness of a whisper or with the energy and intensity of a hurricane, and everything in between. By definition, the bridging of two planes of existence involves a reordering of energy, time, and perception. An infusion of energy occurs as a higher frequency meets with the lower frequency of the physical plane.

A pervasive sense of presence accompanies the powerful shift in the energetic and electrical fields, and the shift is registered by the body and mind and in the immediate surroundings. People report that the air "crackled with electricity" or that "everything shimmered with life. I felt the life force of every molecule of air." Others say, "It was like a huge power surge. Everything glowed with energy and life."

During the visitation, the connection between you and your loved one is absolute. There is a dissolution of the ordinary personal boundaries of inside and outside. Many speak of communication occurring telepathically, with knowledge, experience, and information seeming to come by direct transmission. As the multisensory awareness is open and conscious, much is felt and understood that is far beyond the level of ordinary understanding.

In my many years of collecting visitation stories, I have known of very few people who felt fearful or anxious in any way. I believe this is because of the overwhelming sense of love that usually permeates the experience. Over and over people speak of feeling this love as a substance, a force, at the same time universal and personal. Far beyond experiencing love as an emotion, they know it as the very essence and substance of life.

Commonly, people immediately recognize the one who is seeking to make contact with them. You know immediately and unmistakably that it is Uncle George or Sarah or Grandmother. They are recognizable by their essence and spirit, always highly individual and particular.

Visitations come unannounced. All at once your attention is swept into another world, a larger, more inclusive world that is out of time and space. The experience is so profound that most people have little or no doubt about its reality. "It was the most important thing that has ever happened to me"; "it was the most conscious and wonderful moment of my life. I was more alive in that moment than in all the rest of my life put together." And my favorite, "It was like going from black-and-white to color."

AWAKE AND IN DREAMS

A visitation can occur to someone who is wide awake, in full daylight, in the middle of any activity as well as to one who, lying asleep in bed, is in the midst of dreaming. Still others may experience visitations while in the tender, receptive state between wakefulness and sleep, called the hypnogogic or twilight state.

Over the years, many people have wondered if reunions that occur while one is asleep are "real" visitations. Though many visitations take place during sleep, no one who has had such an experience considers it to be anything like an ordinary dream.

Most people pay little attention to their nightly dreams because, for many of us, ordinary dreams are somewhat vague and fragmented, often confusing and disjointed. Such dreams are not easily understood by the waking mind, filled as they are with strange, symbolic images stitched together in a patchwork of activity. Even those of us who love and attend to our nightly dreams have to work with the mysterious fragments and symbols, trying to translate them into meaningful messages or insights.

A visitation dream is nothing like an ordinary dream. The only commonality is that in each case the body is asleep. A visitation dream is what Carl Jung called a "big dream," a mythic experience that comes to us from the archetypal realm. It speaks to us, from another part of the soul, of something having mythic scale and importance beyond the limitations of our human understanding. It comes from the realm of spirit. Jung called such mythic experiences "numinous," or filled with a sense of holy presence. A pervasive sense of numinosity tells us that something of soul importance is taking place, that we are in sacred territory.

Visitations often do occur in sleep and in the twilight state when the dominant left brain is in abeyance and consciousness is much more permeable. In part, because our brains are functioning differently, we are more available at these times to nonphysical states and the use of our inner sense organs, which allows us to experience more freely the realms of spirit. Sensory modes that are focused and useful in the inner world are not available for many people while awake but are fully functioning in the nonwaking brain states.

Unlike an ordinary dream, which might be *about* someone who has died, in a dream visitation you are dreaming *with* that person, and he or she is aware of having died, of no longer being in physical form, and of the visitation itself. Coming to you consciously with a purpose, the person intends to make meaningful contact. The meeting happens in order to convey to you a message about something important to each of you.

A visitation that takes place in a dreaming state, just as one occurring while wide awake, can fully engage your senses, as you are fully immersed, body, mind, and spirit, in the inner landscape. Because consciousness has unlimited mobility, in a dream as well as while awake, you might stay in one location, or you may be taken to different places and even different times. With your loved one you may go to past or future times and places or to metaphorical landscapes that help the beloved reveal to you the full intention of the message you are to receive. Each landscape may be fully vivified and real to the senses, probably more real than real.

One of the most fascinating aspects of a visitation dream or a waking visitation experience is that it stays in conscious memory in an entirely different way than does an ordinary experience. Characteristically elusive, dreams begin to evaporate the moment we awaken. Their fragile, tentative quality makes remembering them difficult, even in the first few seconds of waking up. A visitation dream, on the other hand, is vividly and profoundly impressed in the conscious memory. It is always said by those who have had a visitation from the afterlife that even many years later it is as though it happened yesterday. The image does not diminish with time. It seems to be stored in a different part of the brain than the memory of other experiences, waking or sleeping.

A visitation is commonly remembered in minute, exquisite detail. Every word, every emotion, every aspect of the vision is there in front of you years later, undiminished, remembered not only by the mind but by the body and heart as well. Filled with that knowing in body, mind, and spirit, you sense that it was somehow more real than any other moment of your life until now.

One person said about a visitation, "If that was just a dream . . . or if that was just a fantasy, then my whole life is a fantastic dream. I don't care what you call it, it was the most wonderful and important thing that has ever happened to me." Others say, "No one could ever convince me that it was just a dream"; "I have never been more certain of anything"; "It was the most real moment of my life before or since."

THROUGH THE AGES

Visitations from the afterlife can come to people at every time of life, at every age. I have heard stories of experiences when people were as young as two years old, still in the crib and not yet speaking (though this seems somewhat rare), as well as from those over a hundred years old, who are themselves nearing the time of passing over. And, of course, every age in between.

Most of the childhood visitations I have heard of came to children after the age of four or five. Children are normally very open and receptive to inner states because they are not yet socialized and limited by concepts and dogmas, be they religious, cultural, or scientific. They are still living close to the core, still connected to the spiritual realms from which they have emerged.

A child who because of an early visitation has the visceral experience of the continuity of life has a secret organizing center within. Such a child develops strength in the awareness, on some level, that her or his life has a larger design and a greater dimension than the scope of ordinary, daily life.

Many adults, in speaking of their childhood visitations, have said that the experience directly influenced their later choices in work, relationships, and spiritual life. Many said that through the visitation they were given the gift early on of knowing that they were cared for, that they were never alone. Many speak of feeling protected and accompanied in life. And they know that life will go on after the life of the body is over. Life choices are different for those among us who have little or no fear of death, who feel not only the presence and protection of the unseen world but also its magic and enchantment.

A visitation at any time in life can inspire a sense of destiny, exerting a pull toward the numinous, like a forgotten memory that tugs at consciousness for remembrance. For many it creates a passionate desire for artistic expression, such as painting, poetry, writing, dancing, sculpture. All of the arts give one a way to call up and express the enchantment and promise of the mystical realm, so powerfully experienced during the visitation.

The stories in this book come from people of all ages, some written by those who are still children at this time, some by adults who experienced a visitation many years ago during childhood. Other stories are of visitations experienced by people in adulthood. At whatever age a visitation comes, its healing and transforming effects often stretch into every aspect of life, changing the way we live and move, sometimes in subtle ways apparent only over time and at other times more dramatically, in the twinkling of an eye.

Chapter 2

Stories of
Love and Healing

People from all over the world, of every age and every walk of life, have contributed to the following collection of stories of visitations from the afterlife. Each writer has generously shared this most precious treasure, knowing that there are others who will find deep and needed healing in these experiences.

Remember as you read these accounts that words alone, no matter how eloquent, do not begin to convey the full reality and impact of the visitation itself—the energy, the enchantment, the power of the shift from the five senses to the inner senses. Words here are indeed the finger pointing to the moon. Imagine telling someone who'd never experienced it what it is like to fall in love.

So, too, a visitation is more than the sum of its parts, and we must look past the failure of words to the energy and essence of each story in order to glimpse its wonder and enchantment. Read with your heart, and allow your soul to drink deeply of the blessing hidden within each story.

A visitation from the afterlife is by definition ineffable and indescribable. One experience may be so subtle that it hardly registers in the conscious mind, while another may come on like fireworks at a parade. One of the most eloquent stories comes from a father explaining why it is almost impossible to write about the visitations of his beloved daughter because they are so very fleeting and insubstantial in any outer way yet so true, so real, so apparent and healing to the heart. These visitations from his child, known with certainty in the heart, barely pass from the glow of feeling into the language of words and thoughts.

The stories found in chapters 3 to 7 are of visitations concerned primarily with grief—the parting, the suffering and anguish of separation, the loss and transition involved in the recent death of a loved one. The central purpose of the visitation itself is the soothing and comforting of grief. These stories have a healing message for those of us in mourning, as they tell us not only that our loved ones are themselves alive and well, but also that we will be with them again when we, too, pass from this life into the next.

In chapters 8 to 14, we find stories of visitations not brought on by recent death or grief. The central focus of these visitations is ongoing concern for the events and circumstances of our daily lives, from the largest life issues, such as vocation, art, marriage, and birth, to the smallest, seemingly trivial daily considerations of recipes and sore throats. These stories tell us that our loved ones in the afterlife know and care about what we are doing and what is happening in our lives and that sometimes they are able to reach through the veil to help when it is needed.

Many of these stories provide evidence of one kind or another. People are told of future events that later happen, of information that is then validated and verified. They receive help with physical, emotional, and spiritual healing and experience loving protection from the other side. Though not given as proof, these experiences help many of us take that leap of faith that visitations are real events that do come from someplace beyond our own imaginings.

When we share life with others, we often have a great affection for the small daily rituals, the endearing, oft-repeated gestures we love for their very ordinariness. These rituals become our private symbols of the intimacy and constancy of our bond with another person. You will see in the following stories that a reunion is frequently the embodiment of this coded, secret language of intimacy known only to those involved. The visitation might consist of one of these simple, defining gestures, which, imprinted on your heart, enables you to recognize and embrace the presence of your love anywhere. Even after death, each of us remains who we are—a particular, richly individualized expression of being.

Most people will tell you that their closest relationships are spiritual in nature. That knowledge is confirmed in these stories. The blessing of a visitation from the afterlife is that a beloved soul returns to give unmistakable assurance that love and caring transcend time and space and last forever.

Chapter 3

Grief:
To Soothe a Grieving Heart

The beloved people and animals with whom you share your life are luminous threads in the tapestry of who and what you are. When they are gone, there is a tear in the very fabric of your being, a wound that, I believe, never fully heals. Somehow, eventually able to go on, we learn how to live with this single greatest irreconcilable fact of life, this wounding that takes us into the deepest layers of ourselves. Touching body, mind, emotion, and spirit, it leaves no part of us unscathed.

Those from beyond may return to draw us away from the downward spiral of grief, to guide us back up into the current of life. Their simple and eloquent messages of continued life and caring bespeak the eternal covenant, the assurance that nothing, not even death, will ever part those who love. "I am here, I love you, and I am always with you," they say. The bond of love is eternal.

Wondering if our loved one is still suffering, if she is sick or wounded or if he is afraid or lonely, can haunt our days and nights. So many times the visitation message is meant to soothe our distressing concerns with the wondrous news of ongoing life, wholeness, and health. Not only is she not suffering anymore, she is living in great happiness and freedom, in beauty beyond human imagination. He is neither lonely nor afraid, surrounded as he is now by the love of friends and family who have passed on before.

Always encouraged to go on with your life, you are assured that the separation, though deeply painful now, is temporary and that soon enough you will be reunited.

The idea that after death we cease to exist, that the heart and mind and soul suddenly end and are no more, greatly wounds us, for it reduces individual life and love to a mere chemical or mechanical process. While revealing that a particular someone is alive and well, every visitation carries the implicit message that all will live on, that life continues for everyone. In the first shimmering, golden moment of awareness that something extraordinary is happening, our personal and existential or spiritual grief begins to heal.

The experience of loss and separation, the desolation that leaves us brokenhearted when special people die, is terribly real. Knowing of the depth and breadth of our suffering, our loved ones may return to help us through this most lonely and difficult passage. Coming to give comfort on our darkest journey, they urge us to behold the precious gift of our time here on earth, knowing that ultimately we will come back together to share our lives in the next world.

A visitation experience may in an instant end the great suffering and pain of grief, yet I have found this to be rare, for healing is a process that continues over time and may never be truly complete. By giving a gentle or not-so-gentle nudge back up toward the surface, a visitation from the afterlife heads us again into the land of the living, from whence the journey of healing may begin. It is a starting point.

The loving concern and presence of those who have passed on may be expressed in a visitation as vivid as fireworks or as celestial music pulsing and dancing with energy. Or it may be a presence so subtle and ineffable that it is forever beyond adequate description—almost outside of perception, certainly beyond thought.

The stories that follow illuminate the compassion, caring, and support expressed for us from the other side. Each story reveals a highly personal encounter, filled with the particular and intimate language of caring that existed between the two people involved. At the same time, each contains a powerful message for us all in the healing of our own grief, both personal and spiritual.

Notice that some people have a single visitation while others experience several, and still others receive visitations that are ongoing over a period of years. Some loved ones, staying close by, return again and again until the one left behind is stronger and more able to go on with life on her own or until there is the support needed to continue.

It is not uncommon for someone to return to a number of bereaved people, family members and friends alike. In one story a young woman, killed in a tragic fall, comes to her devastated father, younger brother, and sister, bringing each comfort enough to bear the impossible reality of her death. Your loved one knows just what is needed to coax you back into engagement with your own life and is able to help you as you move through the transforming fire of healing. Learning to carry your grief, not trying to overcome or banish it, allows you to go forward to lead a full and meaningful life.

Both life and death become inextricable parts of you from that time on. Through the alchemy of that unwelcome fire, you emerge a different being, a vessel put through the flame, wiser and stronger, able now to hold more and greater life. While no one can prevent the suffering that comes to us all in the course of our earthly existence, a visitation blessedly assures that in the darkest hour we are never alone.

Brought back from the greatest darkness

The Blossom in the Garden of My Heart
by Katelyn Ferguson

People have said to me that there is nothing harder than losing a child.

A doctor in the emergency room told me of my son's death. The accident, involving six children, left two young boys dead and another airlifted to the city hospital. The officials needed to know the identity of one of the boys, and I was the only parent they had been able to contact. I was rapidly going into a state of shock when the police escorted me to the mortuary. In the sterile, brightly lit chamber I identified my son's cousin. Next to him, my son's small body lay draped in a brilliant white sheet. The glare increased my shock and disbelief.

As I gazed at his silent, still form, I didn't feel a desire to look or even touch the sheet because I knew he was no longer there. Instead I silently said farewell to his beloved body, one I had so carefully nurtured and faithfully loved so well.

My daughter and son were the most precious treasures in my life. From the very beginnings of their lives, I provided them with the best of foods so they could grow strong and healthy. I was fortunate to be able to nurture my precious children with vegetables and fruits from my large, organic garden. My children were taught to cherish the earth, our "mother," who enriches us with her bounty. While vegetables and fruits nourish the body, it is flowers that make the heart blossom, so I always grew bright and fragrant flowers along the pathways of the garden.

To please us, most children will ask what can they give us. When my children asked me this question, I would always say, "Flowers, smiles, and hugs." Much to my heart's delight, my children would run into my arms, full of smiles, proudly offering me small bouquets of flowers.

After Thaddeus died, I had many anguishing dreams. I remember one that involved an old, nineteenth-century medicine man who drove his horses up to my home in his gaily painted sideshow wagon and declared that he had the "cure-all." He convinced me that his "medicine" could start my son's heart beating again. "That's all that's needed, ma'am."

So I gave him permission to pour his magic elixir down the throat of my lifeless son. Much to my joy, Thaddeus came back to life and I was able to hug him and hear him speak again. My jubilation continued for about five seconds even after I woke up. Suddenly I felt like a freight train had run over me. The harsh reality that nothing could bring him back crashed into me, leaving me breathless.

Thaddeus was dead. This wasn't a bad dream, it was the cruelest waking nightmare. There was no way to bring my son or his cousin back to life.

My grief was immeasurable. My river of tears began as a dark stream of unfathomable sadness. I didn't think anything or anybody could save me from being pulled deeper and deeper into this well from hell, but I was wrong. Someone did—my son.

Thaddeus came to me as I lay awake in bed trying to sleep. Wearing his elfish smile, he took my hand, squeezing it reassuringly as he led me upstairs. As we ascended the stairs, his blond hair became more and more golden and his smile brighter and brighter.

I followed him into a tall, round room bathed in soft, delicate light. The caressing sunlight filtered through long gauze curtains gently undulating from a breeze. I especially noticed that this breeze was coming into the room from all directions. The large, comfortable room did not contain a single piece of furniture, but it seemed perfectly furnished. My body felt light, but everything, including my son, was very three-dimensional. The air was filled with his own special scent.

There was no sense of time, and I knew we were exactly where we should be. I felt soothed, relaxed, and welcomed. My son turned his freckled face (the exact face I would have had if I'd been a boy) up to me with his glowing smile, and in the simple words of a nine-year-old he said to me, "Mom, I'm okay, please don't be sad."

Then, with joyous laughter, he took a small bunch of brightly shining flowers from behind his back and lovingly presented them to me. I returned his laugh as I knelt down to hug his strong, warm body and to bury my face in the sweet flowers.

My son had come to me to give me the only three gifts I had ever asked from him, flowers, smiles, and hugs. Thaddeus's visit reassured me that he was doing "okay" in this gentle, special place. And I knew that he didn't want me to be sad. His single, simple sentence pushed me back up to the surface of life and revived me so I could continue living.

I survived the worst thing that could happen in a mother's life, but I've also experienced the greatest gift, the never-ending love of my child. He is and always will be the blossom in the garden of my heart.

Changed forever, from grief to new life

Cousin Annie
by Damian Michaels

Around the age of seven, I lived for a time with my grandparents at their home in Virginia. During my stay that summer, my grandmother and I went out to the local hospital most mornings where her niece, Annie, was dying of cancer. Annie had many visitors throughout the day, but she always looked forward to spending time with me on those days, as I would go to great lengths to bring laughter or a smile to her face. We had always been close, but during these last months we developed a very special and loving bond.

One morning just after breakfast, I was out by the side of the house playing in the dirt with my matchbox cars. I was on my hands and knees looking down toward the ground when suddenly a warm sensation spread throughout my body and I could not move or turn around at all. It was then that I heard Annie's voice. My life was changed forever.

Annie's voice sounded much stronger than it normally did.

Her presence was so completely real that I thought she'd come home from the hospital to visit us, even though I knew that she was quite ill and couldn't get out of bed. Nonetheless, I thought she was just behind me. And although her voice came from behind and above me, it also felt like it was coming from deep inside me, touching my soul directly from within.

In a voice that was crystal clear, Annie told me that she loved me and would be with me always throughout my life. Suddenly, taken outside of myself, I could see my whole life played out like a movie. I knew exactly who I was and what I would do with my life, and I could see other things on a much larger scale, too, some beautiful and some terrifying.

Suddenly I was taken back to myself, and that warm sensation turned into a cold, empty chill as I felt Annie's presence leaving me. I could even see myself through her eyes, slowly getting smaller and smaller below. Suddenly, I felt totally alone.

Once able to move my body again, I leaped to my feet, screaming Annie's name over and over as I desperately searched the sky for her face. I knew she was there; I could feel her presence and knew she was still there with me but would not say anything because I somehow knew she couldn't. Grief-stricken and overwhelmed with a great sadness, I started to cry. I then became scared and ran into the house looking for my grandmother.

I found her talking on the phone to the hospital. Quite upset by this time, I was crying and screaming about what had just happened in the yard. When my grandmother got off the phone, she told me Annie had died only moments earlier.

That was the day my real life began.

Three stories of grief-stricken family members blessed by a visit from their beloved Sharon. First, her father . . .

In the Stillness of an Open Heart

by Terry Stout

My daughter, Audrey, stood in the doorway watching me for several minutes before she knelt beside my bed to awaken me. It was the middle of the night, and she had to tell me the hardest thing that I would ever hear. My younger daughter, Sharon, had fallen three stories from a fire escape to the concrete below. Several agonizing days later, she died.

Early the next morning in my hotel room, everything was quiet as I slowly awakened. Halfway between waking and sleeping, I rolled onto my back with my eyes still closed. My mind had already begun racing with the raw emotion of the past few days, and I was desperate to find some peace in that moment. I struggled to quiet my clamoring mind long enough to still my broken heart.

Then, in the very midst of my turmoil, I clearly heard a noise that instantly brought all my senses into sharp focus, like a deer who, sensing motion, raises its head, points its ears in that direction, and remains very, very still. Every fiber of my being listened intently. Each time my mind began to wander, to question, or even engage a thought, I would clearly hear an increasingly louder and stubbornly insistent "shhh!" Then I felt, rather than saw, an image of my daughter Sharon "shushing" me to stillness.

Now she definitely had my attention, and all those noisy, random thoughts dissipated in the wind of her "shhh." In that instant my mind dropped, and all that was left of me was a wide open heart. As I finally entered that place of absolute stillness, in that same instant, everything became a brightness.

There are no adequate words to describe what this brightness was like. It was a brilliance that illuminated everything but blinded nothing. The feeling was of the deepest love and most profound peace. And, once again, I felt my daughter's presence. Without words, there was total communication, a kind of knowing through feeling, as if we were one being, all mixed together with complete and instantaneous understanding. A communion.

I don't know how long this continued. It could have been a brief moment or a lifetime. There was no time.

Then, in an explosion of relief, exuberance, and powerfully overwhelming joy, I felt, heard, experienced my daughter's resoundingly triumphant cry of "Yes!" within, around, and through me. This joyful cry so completely startled me that I was thrust immediately back into my tingling body, lying on the bed in the pale morning light that now filled the room.

And I was at peace.

Sharon lovingly came also to soothe and comfort her sister, Audrey, and her grieving eight-year-old brother, Josh. Since that time, each of us has certainly had a roller-coaster ride with grief, but there is a knowledge from the experience that has never left. It continues to reshape the way we as individuals and as a family walk in this world.

Bringing comfort to her younger brother, eight-year-old Josh

My Sister Sharon

by Josh Stout

In my dream I saw a huge crowd of people, like all the people in the United States, being held by a giant.

My sister Sharon was in that crowd and escaped to come be with me. We got into a car and started riding. Then my mom's cell phone rang, and I picked it up to listen. The voice on the phone was Sharon's, saying she was sorry that she had had to leave me. She was sorry if she had failed me by leaving so soon.

My sister still loves me and knows how much I miss being with her like before. I know she's sorry that we aren't together right now.

Two sisters affirm their bond across eternity

My Baby Sister

by Audrey Stout

After Sharon died, everything around me seemed so surreal. Life became unfamiliar as I felt more and more lost. Constantly looking for her, increasingly depressed, I dreaded the coming of morning after my long sleepless nights.

One afternoon as I lay on my bed staring up at the ceiling, I had a vision of Sharon. As the ceiling started to change shape, there appeared a face that I could soon see was my sister's face, with the radiant, sparkling eyes that only she had.

Sharon whispered, "It's okay. I love you and I'm still here with you. You and I share an eternal bond and a closeness that can *never* be broken. We'll always be a big part of each other."

Sharon's words and presence brought me profound comfort in knowing that even though our relationship had changed its form, she never really left me at all. We carry each other in our souls.

The loss of the relationship we once shared here still leaves a painful rawness in my heart, but I am able now to go on, knowing that my baby sister, Sharon, is alive and that we will one day be together again.

Because she is the one who listens; a grandmother's poem

For Julian

by Miranda Pope

There is a fruit of which it's said, "it slips its skin," and so you did.

And I saw you skipping through the funeral home trying to get someone's attention.

And weeks later you came to me saying, "Tell my mom I'm okay!"

I asked you then, "Why did you choose to come to me?"

And you answered, "You are the one who listens."

I listened again as your spirit played around me while I sat in my car on the street waiting, and I said, "Julian, I know you're happy now, but I worry about the drowning, that you were scared and choking . . ."

And suddenly, I was transported to the bottom of the blue-green water and felt your calm and wonder as you watched the sunlight dancing on the sides of the pool.

I felt no fear.

Once more, another time you emerged from the bubbling creek as I sat beside it playing my drum and singing. You reached up and held my face in your dear, dear hands. I felt your sweetness, and I thought to myself, "This is why it's so hard for her, his mother. He was unconditional love."

Later, touching your mother's face just so, I asked her, "Did Julian touch your face that way?"

And she breathed, "Yes," and cried.

When I visited just a week before you drowned, we teased and rolled on your bed, and when it was time for me to go home you said to your mother, "Tell my Gramma Mira she has to stay for thirty days."

And so I have, little one, and will again thirty, and thirty more until your hundredth day.[1]

And then, I will let you go.

Nightmares of fear and grief end with the assurances of her young friend

On Another Plane
by Sandy Chappel-Crume

When I was a fifth grader in Texas, my friend Ann had a boyfriend named Hartzell. His friend Ronnie was my boyfriend, so the four of us spent a lot of time together, meeting at the Saturday movies and after school at the drugstore, just hanging out a lot.

I really was a fan of Hartzell's. There was a great sweetness about him, and even at the age of ten he listened to our problems and cared about everyone else. He was special with teachers, parents, and his many, many friends. Everyone loved Hartzell.

One Sunday when Hartzell and his parents went on a picnic he found a strange-looking metal ball, which he brought home. Then one day, of course curious about what might be inside the mysterious object, Hartzell took it outside to the family storage shed, where he put a screwdriver into the seam and hit it hard with a hammer. Hartzell was instantly blown to smithereens. It turned out that the ball was a bomb left over from World War I training maneuvers.

All of Hartzell's schoolmates had a very hard time with this gruesome tragedy. Everyone was traumatized and terrified while also hungry for every horrible detail of what had happened to their

[1] An Indonesian ceremony, this *selamatan* honors the departed as the soul leaves the earthly plane.

friend. In those days of the 1950s, there were no grief counselors, and in a small town therapists were an oddity, so everyone dealt with the situation the best that they could.

I was having terrible nightmares on a nightly basis. Sometimes Hartzell was blown into a million pieces; then I would be the one blown to smithereens; sometimes it was other people. Frequently I woke up screaming or crying, always utterly anguished and terrified.

Then one night I had a perfectly clear dream, so vivid that I can see it clearly to this day. It wasn't like a usual dream at all and nothing like the nightmares. In it, Hartzell and I were talking and I was telling him how upset and grief-stricken I was and how much I missed him now. Behind him was an airplane. Hartzell looked directly at me, right into my eyes, and said "Sandy, don't worry about me! I'm just on another plane."

The nightmares stopped.

A grieving boy now knows that he is never alone

I Am Always with You

by Chris Holmes

My mom had lung cancer for two years, and after every round of chemotherapy we kept hoping she'd beat it, but finally she didn't. She died as I held her hand and told her, "Mom, I love you."

My mom and I had always had a close connection when it came to spirituality. She supported me when I got into spiritual activities, like working with a pendulum, even though everyone else in the family was skeptical. The time that I saw my guardian angel and told everyone what happened, Mom was the only one who believed me. So it makes sense to me that she wanted to visit me after she died.

My mom's visit to me came two or three weeks later, at about 2:15 in the morning when I was sleeping. I woke up because I felt her presence in the room, but I was unable to move or open my eyes because it felt like my body was still sleeping.

It was my mom's voice, saying sweetly, "I'll always love you. I

miss you, honey. Please know that I'm always right here with you."
When she stopped speaking to me, I could still feel her presence.

It was very hard to open my eyes, but when I finally did, I couldn't
see anything unusual, and even though I couldn't get back to sleep
for a long time I felt more at peace.

I still really miss my mom, but since she came to visit me that
night I have felt a little better because I do know that she's with me
and that I'll see her again someday.

*A woman and her husband, sharing a moment with their son,
know that he lives on*

The Voice of Love
by Vivian Husted

We were almost never apart during those many years that I carried him around on my hip all his waking hours. Born with a congenital hip deformity and in splints for the first year of his life, my
son, Richard, and I had a particularly close bond. It took a long
time, but he finally learned to walk.

At twenty-four Richard had his first job after college, working
during the day while his wife, a nurse, worked evenings. He was at
home with their baby daughter in the evening, and every night
before the baby went to bed, he put her in a backpack and the two
of them went out for a walk.

On one particular night when Richard started out to go walking,
the neighbors wanted to play with the baby for a while, so, leaving
her with them, he headed out alone. Though it was not raining or
storming, Richard had gone only a short distance when he was
struck by lightning. The rain came afterward.

Our family was devastated by his death.

One night about a month later, I got up in the middle of the night
to go to the bathroom, and no sooner than I had gotten back into
bed than the bedroom door opened wide and my son, Richard,
stuck his head into the room.

"Hi, Mom," he said laughing and closing the door.

The next morning when I told my husband that I had seen and heard Richard during the night, he insisted I had been dreaming. I insisted I had been wide awake!

While preparing to go to bed one night about a month after that, my husband was in the bedroom while I was in the kitchen preparing the coffeepot for the morning when the telephone rang. I answered it in the kitchen, and my husband, at the same time, picked up the phone in the bedroom.

"Hi, whatcha doin'?" Richard asked, just as he'd always asked whenever he'd called us before his death.

"What do you mean, what am I doing?" I said without thinking. "I'm fixing the coffeepot as usual this time of night."

Richard laughed heartily and hung up!

Walking into the bedroom, I asked my husband if he recognized the voice on the phone. With tears in his eyes, he said, "Yes, yes, I did. It was Richard!" There was no question about it, it was Richard.

From that moment on, my husband knew in his heart, as I did, that our beloved son was alive and well, and we both began to feel more able to live with the terrible pain and nearly unbearable grief that had overtaken us the night of his death. So certain were we that there is a life after this life that we even made a promise that whichever of us died first, we would try to reach the other if possible, to let the other know about life beyond this world.

Four years later my husband died suddenly while we were on vacation.

His presence is with me much of the time since then. Assuring me that he would stay with me as long as I needed him, my husband said, "I just changed my ZIP code."

A lost and sorrowful child in need of love and support has visitations from her aunt

The Loving Legacy of Aunt Libby
by Marlane Taylor

My Aunt Lib doted on me. Libby, as everyone called her, was my mother's older sister. I was a young child then, and she and I were inseparable. Whenever she came to visit, I was the adored one in her eyes. We walked woods and pastures together, she carrying me in her arms across creeks and through fields of flowers. Together we watched the birds and butterflies as they danced in the sunlight. Aunt Lib was my angel if there ever was one, and I loved her more than anyone on this earth. She was everything to me.

Aunt Libby, married to a handsome fellow who was away at war, was expecting their first child sometime in July. The last time I saw her was when she took me to the country fair on that Fourth of July. Dressed up in a navy blue dress with a white lace collar, a blue hat, and blue and white spectator pumps, she held my hand as we walked through the golden grass in the field among all the booths covered with red, white, and blue bunting. Fireworks, games, and music, my hand in hers—it was a wonderful day, and I loved every minute of being with her. My aunt was the joy of my life.

The next day we got word that Aunt Lib was on her way to the hospital to have the baby, so we drove to her small town near the fairgrounds. By the time we arrived, Aunt Lib had already passed away during childbirth. Though she had died from suffocation due to food aspiration, her baby girl was perfect.

What happened to my Aunt Lib? Where is she? I looked everywhere, in every window and every room where Aunt Lib might be, but she was nowhere to be found. All I could see was the hospital's green walls and floors and dark, empty rooms. People were crying. I only wanted to see my Aunt Lib, yet no one would answer me when I begged and pleaded to know where she was.

I asked again and again. I asked everyone, "Where is my Aunt Lib?" But everyone ignored my questions, spoke in hushed tones, and told me nothing at all about Aunt Lib's death, thinking it would disturb me, just a small girl, to know the truth.

All I really knew and understood was that my favorite person in the entire world, in all the universe, my angel, was suddenly gone and that I would never, ever see her again.

How wrong I was!

Not long afterward, Aunt Libby came to me dressed all in white. Holding me high up above her head, we danced and twirled together in the sunlight. I could feel the warmth of the sun on my back and the feel of her hands holding me up. I could smell the fragrant dried grass under our feet. Her radiant, loving smile shone deeply into my eyes, and I drank it in, filling my utterly broken spirit with her love.

After that first glorious day, Aunt Libby came to me at night in my room. Each night she gently placed her hands on my head and stroked my hair as if to soothe my broken heart.

"I will never leave you," she would always say, looking at me with infinite love. "How could I?" Promising me that she would always watch over and take care of me, she said that she would come to me if ever I needed her.

My deepest sorrow was slowly transformed as Aunt Libby came to me every night until I was about thirteen years old. Only much, much later did I realize that other people did not have such experiences, such visitations. Aunt Lib was with me because I needed her so much during those years, and it was not until I was about thirteen that I became strong enough to go on without her. Then she began to fade away, until she came no more.

To this day, I could paint her face from memory—that is how clearly and vividly I remember the nights Aunt Libby was there by my side, keeping me safe until I could begin to live without her gentle guidance, love, and protection.

*A child who was a blessing in life comes to his godmother
in her sorrow*

The Sweetest Sound

by Edna Wilson

When the doctor told his parents that my godson, Calder, had been born with a rare congenital disorder affecting his lungs and throat and that he would certainly die within a few weeks, his parents found another doctor. Then they set about giving their beloved little boy a full life in the four years he survived, making medical history in the process.

Calder exerted a profound influence on all who knew him. He seemed to bring out the truth in people just by being himself. The Paul Winter Consort gathered around his bed to serenade him and to learn from him. The family minister referred to him as "a little horizontal Buddha."

He was unable to walk or talk, but without ever speaking even a single word, Calder developed his intellect to an extraordinary degree. He played Mozart ("Twinkle, Twinkle, Little Star") on his keyboard at eighteen months, began reading almost immediately, and became a computer whiz. By the time his lungs finally gave out and he could go no further, he was reading at a fifth-grade level. It was two months after his fourth birthday.

The day Calder died, his father called me with the news just as I was on my way out the door to attend a session at my dream group. The leader of the group used a meditation technique that day designed simply to take people into the relaxation that facilitates dream work. I had not previously experienced anything out of the ordinary while in this kind of gentle meditation.

On this day, as she directed us to visualize a gardenlike setting, in my grieving heart I found myself asking, "My dearest Calder, where are you?"

Suddenly, I distinctly heard a child's voice, innocent and sweet, saying, "I'm whole. I'm happy. I'm healthy." The message repeated sweetly, several times.

My heart rejoiced! I knew with absolute certainty that it was Calder and that I was hearing his beautiful voice for the first time.

As gently as a breeze, a beloved daughter stays close
to her grieving parents

The Touch of Grace
by Cristóvão Nobre

Yes, we had a daughter, Monica, who passed into the spiritual world eight years ago when she was ten. My wife, Cleia, and I have many times felt her presence; however, these are very subtle and personal experiences and perhaps not even ones that can be told.

When trying to speak of our experience, I have come to realize that it is almost impossible to do. We have had many subtle impressions or perceptions that have made us feel that our beloved daughter still dwells among us. These impressions have been such gentle, subtle signs, shown to us many times through the same smile on another child's face or a child's eyes looking at us in the same way our daughter's eyes gazed upon us. Or we might hear Monica's clear voice amid the screams and shouts of her siblings and other children of her age as they were playing.

Sometimes, when my wife was feeling deeply sorrowful and overwhelmed by the sadness of missing her daughter, some other child would quite suddenly come to hug and kiss my wife without any apparent reason and then again go away, as if an angel had told him or her to come do that quickly.

We also have had several dreams of Monica, in which we hug her so perceptibly that we still feel a tender pressure of her embrace in our chest and arms as we awaken. Yes, we have had hundreds of these soft and very tender signs over these years. They are like a quick and mild breeze; we cannot predict their occurrence, and they seem so fragile and insubstantial when conveyed to others. But these gentle, indescribable moments have given us tremendous comfort in our unfathomable grief.

It is true that no one of these experiences is so special, impressive, or dramatic that it can be meaningfully related to others. Many people could even call them a product of our imagination. We are sorry that we cannot express them better or make them more apparent or noticeable, but I presume that it is because they are not intended to be proof but only to give us comfort during our temporary separation from our beloved daughter.

We are reminded that the Lord's grace is often so subtle and so ineffable that it cannot in reality ever be fully communicated to another person and that we are instead to take in that moment of grace down into the deepest chamber of our hearts. We can only hope then that we may bless others by who we are, not by what we are able to say with our words.

We know that Monica's presence comes again to us with the kind permission of the Lord in order to comfort us during these terrible times of our grief, as an assurance that love is a strong attraction that does not end with death.

Chapter 4

Good-bye:
Saying Good-bye, for Now

When I say good-bye to someone I love it is with the fond hope that our parting is temporary, that our leave-taking is for now, until the next time, whether the next time is in an hour or a day, next week or next year. And, while you are away from me, know always that my good wishes go with you wherever you go and whatever you do. As I say the word *good-bye,* it is with my sometimes silent but always present prayer that God's grace be with you throughout your journey until I see your dear face again.

A profound ritual act of daily life, saying good-bye is filled with symbolic meaning and spiritual intention. Anytime we are truly present as we say farewell it becomes a moment when the world stops and, focusing our whole attention on each other, we acknowledge and honor each other, our bond, and this parting. In this most ordinary of daily acts, which may last only a few seconds, we make conscious our caring connection and give each other the blessing hidden inside every loving farewell.

Saying good-bye is so important to us that it should come as no surprise that it is the central purpose of many beautiful visitations from the afterlife. In story after story from around the world, from ancient times until the present, one of the most common themes is the visitation that occurs just at the time of death or very soon after, as the loved one passes out of this world and into the next. Seeking us out at such a momentous time to say farewell honors the deep bond of love and lives so richly shared.

For many, the visitation serves as the first news of the death of their loved one, before it comes through more ordinary channels such as telephones, letters, or newspapers. This most intimate communication says, I want to tell you myself that I am embarking on a journey and I am here to say good-bye, for now.

Several of the touching stories in this chapter are of this kind. In many of these, because the death was not anticipated, the experience came unexpectedly to the person receiving the visitation.

Then there are stories in which the farewell comes later, after the funeral. Here the purpose is to lovingly ask the grieving person to let go. The loved one says, "Release me, say farewell, for now, so that I can go on with my journey and you can go on with your life until it is the time for us to meet again." The suggestion is that a person's ongoing anguish can keep both people bound by a constricting energetic tie, which serves the highest good of neither. Releasing allows both to go forward, to fulfill their individual destinies in this life and the life of the hereafter.

We each have a soul destiny, and we need freedom to experience and express those things necessary for the fulfillment of our unique vision. By releasing those with whom we share a bond of love, in this life or the life after, we do not bind or limit one another; rather, our love gives freedom and support in the full trust that the heart's connection is eternal and cannot be broken or lost.

The greater message of every visitation is that life continues after the death of the body and that we will be together again. You can trust that our separation is temporary. Just as you carry me wherever you go, I shall carry you. A visitation from the afterlife tells us all that, for those who love, good-bye means good-bye, for now, until we meet again.

*Saying good-bye honors special friendship while giving needed
assurance that all is well*

Hill Country
by Michael Drummond Davidson

The hill country of northern Mississippi is as about as pic-turesque as it comes. Huge tracts of pine and hardwood forests pat-tern the countryside. Rough hillocks and fertile bottoms transverse hundreds of square miles with hardly any settlements or roads. There is nothing but forest trail and fire tract and the occasional sunken wagon road from Civil War times. Upon these hills the bountiful Mississippi white-tailed deer and black razorback hog make their homes and trails.

Young Chris Stewart was native to these parts. At a strapping eighteen years old, Chris was an accomplished hunter and tracker. In a state where the deer population is triple the human population, such skills are important, for they give opportunity to hone a young person's intuition and self-confidence. These are qualities that can only be self-taught, earned through a keen mind and a heart open, in direct contact with the wilderness. For his young age Chris was a teacher. Younger children looked up to him, as he made them feel included and valued for their contribution.

With his gift of gab, southern drawl, and handsome good looks, he could, as they say down here, "talk the chicken off the bone" and effectively did so, charming young and old alike with fishing and hunting stories. His good looks were not for naught, and when he went steady with a girl for the first time last year it was no surprise that they made a handsome couple.

Chris and my wife were first cousins, so we always saw a good bit of each other. I was always impressed with his maturity and his ability to communicate directly with adults. We would hunt in the fall and early winter, then fish in the spring and summer. I always felt honored to hunt with him, despite his youth. Even though I was a bit older, we were great friends.

In early spring I was returning home from Chicago, from working thirty-three stories up on a scaffold hanging off the Chicago Tribune Building. For six weeks I'd been subject to the winds and storms of Lake Michigan, along with the broken-nose eloquence of the labor foreman. I was ready to come home, to be with my family, hang with my hunting dogs, kick back, and do a little fishing with Chris.

My wife had planned a surprise birthday party for me on my return and had the house festooned with spring flowers. The trees were done up in twinkle lights. She'd invited the whole neighborhood over to eat a barbecued pig that Chris had slow-cooked overnight on coals in the ground. There was a fiddler, too.

I arrived home and was completely surprised by the party. We waltzed and two-stepped, drank punch, and partied half the night. Everyone I wanted to see was there except Chris. His mother and father were there, enjoying themselves and reassuring me Chris would be along after he dropped his girl off from an afternoon excursion. So we carried on and had a great time before calling it a night and retiring to our homes.

Just before turning off the light, I remarked to my wife about Chris's absence. It wasn't like him to miss a party, especially not my birthday party. She reminded me that he was with his girl, and, well, anything can change your plans at that age. With that, I turned off the light and fell into deep sleep.

The next thing I knew the phone was ringing. It rang and rang, so finally I answered it, still groggy from sleep. It was Chris.

"Chris," I said, "where are you?" He started in saying he was sorry and went on in his usual charming way. He was sorry that he had missed my birthday party but assured me that he was all right, in a great place, and didn't want me to worry about him. Again he said that he was "all right," using a reassuring tone that was of the clearest assurance and joy. The joy in his voice brought a smile to my sleepy face. He spoke as if he were in the room with me, and I was assured that he was fine and that I would see him later. We hung up, I rolled over feeling great, and closed my eyes to go back to sleep.

Then, just a few minutes later, still the middle of the night, the phone rang again. I picked it up, thinking was probably Chris again, but it wasn't. It was my wife's mom.

"He's dead! He's dead!" was all she could say.

Thinking she meant her husband, I said, "Calm down. What are you talking about?"

"Chris—he's dead, killed in a car wreck two hours ago. Please, can you come over to the house?"

By this time I was shaking my wife and putting her on the phone with her mother while I dressed. Already, I was struggling with the fact that it could not be true that Chris was dead two hours, because I had just talked to him a few minutes ago. My mind was racing, trying to make sense out of Chris's call. What had he called about? And now this cruel nightmare, which was not going away.

This was not a dream. I was shaking.

The nightmare became even more real upon entering the dead boy's house and witnessing the overwhelming tragedy that had befallen his shocked, grief-stricken family.

For the next week and month thereafter I was swept up in all the things that had to be done in such a crisis. I never really talked about the phone call from Chris except with my wife. I just did whatever I could to reassure everyone that "Chris is all right. He's in a good place."

I'm just so grateful that on his way into the next life, Chris stopped in for a while to say good-bye.

God, how I miss him.

Saying farewell for now, a husband and wife assure each other that they will be well until they meet again

Somewhere, My Love
by Elizabeth Johnson

Herman and I had parted that morning with our usual good-bye kiss, and I did not see my husband again until he was prepared for burial.

He had gone quail hunting the day before, and, pleased with his luck and in wonderful good spirits, he said, "Let's have a bird supper and then go into town to see a rerun of *Dr. Zhivago.*" So when I finished teaching at the high school that day I hurried home to prepare the special supper and get ready for our evening out.

"Something has happened to Herman!" my sister said as she came running into the kitchen where I was preparing the quail. "He collapsed while on the golf course and died." I was stunned. Stupefied! Filled with disbelief. Herman had had a massive brain hemorrhage just as he got into the golf cart to drive to the next hole. Death was instant, and nothing could be done.

After the burial, when everyone was gone, I was by myself for the first time since Herman's death, and I suddenly felt the vast, gaping hole in my life. I decided to go out to the cemetery, to be alone for some quiet time to try to take in what had happened. For the longest time, I stood there, looking down at the new grave and the flowers. When I finally raised my eyes and looked skyward, I saw Herman!

Life-size and fully clothed in his favorite gray slacks and light gray shirt, Herman was looking quizzically at me, asking, "Are you all right, Elizabeth? Will you be all right?" Half walking, half floating, he was only a little distance away but well out of my reach.

Clearly, Herman was deeply torn between staying here with me and going on, and he was looking at me for assurance.

"Go!" I cried out. "It's all right, Herman, I will be all right. Goodbye for now. I release you, my dear love, not because I want to, but because I must. I know that I must turn the page and start a new chapter in my life. And I know that you, too, must go on."

Over and over again in my heart I said, "Thank you, Lord, for allowing me to have this special vision and this precious time with my dear husband." It was such a wonderful thing that was happening. Herman needed to say good-bye and could not go forward on his journey until he knew that I would be all right, until I said farewell and released him to go on.

After lingering there for a while longer, I decided to go back home. Once at the house, sitting there at my kitchen window, I could still see Herman slowly, slowly floating upward farther and farther away into the twilight. Looking back in my direction now and again, he gradually disappeared.

I deeply treasure this very precious and unexpected blessing, which has comforted me greatly through the years. I know now that our love spans all circumstances. It was the good-bye we didn't get to say. It was the blessed assurance of Herman's love and concern and of our eventual reunion somewhere, sometime, somehow.

At the moment of farewell, a young Dutchman is opened to the spiritual dimension of life, seeing for himself that death is a passage from this world into the next

To Say Good-bye

by Jojan Jonker

Around seven in the morning I woke up when I heard the telephone ringing. I was twenty-two years old and staying over for a weekend with my girlfriend at her parents' home. Sitting up in bed, I immediately saw my dear grandmother standing in a corner of the bedroom! She was visible from the top of her head to halfway down her chest, and she appeared light gray in color and a little transparent. She was laughing as she stood there waving happily at me. I waved back.

Excited now, I woke up my girlfriend shouting, "Look! Look, my grandmother, over there!" I pointed to the corner of the bedroom. "In the corner! Look!" But she couldn't see anything and became a little frightened. It was then that Grandmother just faded away into thin air.

In the meantime my girlfriend's mother had answered the telephone and come into our room to say that it was my father wanting to speak with me. I took the phone, and when my father said that he had something important to tell me, I told him that I already knew what it was—that my grandmother had just died.

It seemed that she had fallen out of her bed and broken her arm. She was taken to the hospital, where it was discovered that she had internal bleeding that could not be stopped. Because it was found too late, she died.

All of this had occurred very suddenly while I was away from home, and I was unaware of these things happening. The last time I had seen my grandmother she had been quite well.

After that I didn't mourn the passing of my dear grandmother, because I knew that she was alive and I had seen with my own eyes that she is happy. I still thank her for taking the time to show herself to me and to say good-bye, for now.

This experience became one of the greatest importance in the direction of my own spiritual life.

Bidding his son farewell, a father asks a special favor

The Hunting Trip
by David Nealey

I was in my lab that morning, and, after pouring myself a cup of tea, I headed back to my private office. As I did, I was pushed through the doorway, almost spilling the tea. I put down the cup, intending to let whoever it was know that I didn't appreciate the shove. Before I could turn around, though, the door closed and the room was completely filled with the brightest light I have ever seen. The light was concentrated mostly in front of the door. It radiated a warmth, but it was an emotional warmth rather than heat as from sunlight. Without really knowing why, I said, "Dad?"

Dad started speaking immediately, not aloud but in my mind, certainly going too fast for me to understand. Realizing that, he seemed to pause to collect the chaotic electricity that filled the room. When he started talking again, he was much more calm. Dad began by saying that he loved me, and as he did a wave of love broke over me like an avalanche. In the minute before he said it, I knew that he was dead. He then told me that he had died while out on his yearly hunting trip.

"When?" I cried out inside and found myself praying that I was asleep. Let this be a dream!

"About an hour ago. They're just getting my body back to the van." He paused very briefly as I took in the whole picture. He went on, "There is something that I want you to do for me. Please, son. Right away. It's your mother. Please go over to the house so that you'll be with her when they call. It will be a good hour before they can phone with the news. Your Uncle Albert"— my mother's brother who was part of the hunting club—"will call her around eleven.

"You've got to be there!" he said with urgency. "Beth is going to need you there when she hears the news." I asked him if I should tell her first, myself. He said no, that it was for Albert to do.

Dad assured me that he was fine, saying that dying had not been painful at all. "Sort of interesting." he said. "I am alive, but I can't say much more about it than that. I have a feeling that I will go on, someplace, from here." He paused and then said, "This is a pretty good joke on me." Dad had been an atheist to the core and quite vocal about it. A scientist all the way, he had believed in no God and certainly no afterlife, and that was all there was to it. He had not had a speck of tolerance for any other viewpoint.

Leaving the office immediately, I drove to my mother's home about twenty minutes away. On the way I quite simply could not imagine how I was going to act normally until my uncle's call came in. Just as I pulled into the drive I was filled—and I do mean filled, like an empty bottle being filled up with water—with serenity.

With no effort of my own, I was able to greet my mother just as always. She took me in hand to show me the new flowers in the garden, and then we had our morning tea. Throughout this time I was in a state of utter peace.

When the call finally came, Mum was devastated, as Dad knew she would be. The uncanny peace and serenity that I felt lasted for several weeks and really enabled my mother, and me, to get through the difficult days that followed.

About two years later, my mother described to me a visit from Dad that had taken place about a month earlier, there in the garden.

She and my father had been together. Embracing her warmly, he told her that he missed her and promised that they would be together again. Well and happy himself, Father told Mother that he wanted her to go on with her life. (She'd been very depressed since his death.) Mum said never before had she felt such love.

"'Good-bye for now, dear Beth.'" Tears filled her eyes as she spoke his parting words. "'Be well. Before you know it we shall be together again.'"

My mother had been hesitant to tell me this happened because, my being a scientist, she felt that I wouldn't believe that it had really occurred. She said that it was more real than anything that had ever happened to her, before or since. No one could convince her other-wise.

Of course, I said that she didn't need to convince me of anything at all, and I told her the whole story about Dad's parting visit to me at the time of his passing. To this day, I recall every word that Dad said and even the way the light fell on different objects in the room. It was the most remarkable few minutes of my entire life.

The gift of knowing that she is never alone

A Gentle Breeze

by Barbara Estep

I knew that my grandmother was very sick, but I didn't really understand that she was near death. At sixteen, I was her only grandchild, and we were very, very close. My happiest childhood memories are the summers we spent together.

That night, in the middle of the night, as I was asleep at her house, I was startled awake by a vision of my grandmother hovering above me in the pitch black. I felt her gently touching my shoulder. A breeze filled the room, and it suddenly became very cold, almost freezing.

"Barbara," Grandmother clearly called out my name, "know that I love you very, very much." Then she was gone.

And that was the end of the vision. I started sobbing and ran to the front bedroom to find my mother, to tell her about what had happened, but my mother wasn't anywhere in the house. I became very scared. It was all so completely real. About twenty minutes later the phone rang, and it was my mother calling from the hospital to tell me my grandmother had died a little while before, just about the time that I saw her hovering above me in the dark.

I knew then with absolute certainty that it wasn't a dream, and suddenly all my fear went away and I was filled with a sense of peace and joy. My grandmother, as she passed through to the other side, came to me to say good-bye, for now.

It was one of the defining moments of my life, lifting the veil between life and death. Because of her visitation, I never grieved in the traditional sense about Grandmother's passage, though I have missed her loving presence every day of my life since then, even today. There is nothing that anyone could ever say that would convince me that my visitation was only a dream. It was the most real moment of my life.

Good-bye is not the end, but another beginning

On the Square
by Roni Chernin

Nine thousand miles from home, I was just seventeen and living on a kibbutz in Israel. On a typical warm, sunny day, as I was crossing the square (a grassy circular area around which the main buildings of the kibbutz were clustered), I suddenly stopped. There, right in front of me, was my grandfather, floating just a little off the ground! He looked fully solid as he stood there smiling broadly at me.

Feeling a little confused, I wondered if I was imagining him there, while at the same time I noticed a deep feeling of acceptance and completeness within me. Yes, this really was happening. No fear, no confusion, only the greatest sense of peace.

Standing there, as though waiting for something to happen, I had no idea how much time passed. Then, after a while, Grandpa, still smiling, shimmered away and was gone, rather much like the "beam me up" on *Star Trek*. At the time, I thought this was a little strange and that my imagination must be pretty active. Certainly curious, I went on with my day.

Sometime later, I was hurried out of my workplace by a young child who was jumping up and down excitedly, saying, "Come now, come now! You have a phone call from the United States!"

"Sit down." It was my father. With his first words, everything became clear to me.

"It's Grandpa, isn't it," I said, a statement more than a question.

My father gave me the details of my grandfather's passing. I asked him when it happened, and it turned out that my grandfather probably came to say good-bye to me within minutes after his death.

This was my secret, and I held it from my family for many years because I thought they wouldn't believe me. But finally, when my grandmother was starting to die, I told her about Grandpa's coming to me on the square that day to say good-bye as he left this world so many years before.

Grandmother wasn't surprised at all. She said, "Yes, your grandfather and I have talked together several times since he died." My grandmother told me of the things that she and Grandpa talked about, and we both came away from that conversation with the implicit knowing that death isn't really the end of life at all. Good-bye is not the end.

The heart can begin to heal

Billy Lee

by Walter Stewart

I was staying in Bernalillio, New Mexico, with a Native American shaman from the Picuris Pueblo. I was still grieving badly from the loss of my best buddy and traveling companion, Billy. This shaman suggested that I needed to say good-bye to Billy, and I agreed to meet to get some kind of closure and move on. So the shaman placed me in his kiva, and the cedar was lit. I faced the east and asked Billy to come to me so I could let him go and get some closure on this.

I lay down facing east, and I fell asleep and went into the dream-time. In my vision I found myself floating and then climbing a small chrome ladder up higher and higher into the clouds. I looked down and could not see the ground. I just kept climbing.

Then there was a door off to the left.

I was scared. It was an awkward leap to get the door open and climb in. I felt compelled to do it, though. When I made the jump, I found myself inside the cab of an eighteen-wheeler. I was driving and shifting gears when Billy, who was sitting shotgun, began complaining about how I was shifting the gears. He was cussing and being himself, just like the old days when we traveled cross-country. I did the same back.

Good-bye, Billy, my friend.

With a reminder of what is truly important in life

Spotted Fawn's Farewell

by Stanley Krippner

While attending a parapsychology conference in Mexico, I had a dream that I had arrived at drummer Mickey Hart's ranch. As I drove in, Rolling Thunder, the great Native American healer and teacher, and his friends were driving out. He had a sober expression on his face, as did the other members of his entourage. I asked, "Where is Spotted Fawn?"

Rolling Thunder turned his head slightly toward the back of the truck, where I saw a wooden coffin strapped to the floor. I knew that it contained the earthly remains of his beloved wife, my old friend, Spotted Fawn.

Just as I was waking up, I heard Spotted Fawn's voice saying to me, "You know, I won't be seeing you anymore." I knew that she was saying good-bye.

Upon arriving back in the United States, I learned that she had passed over that very night. I felt grateful that I had spent so much time with her during her final weeks of life. Indeed, this was the message of Spotted Fawn's visitation:

Life is fickle. One never knows how long it will stay before making its departure, sometimes in a leisurely fashion, sometimes in a manner quite agonizing, and at other times in a style that is abrupt. Spend time with people you love, and demonstrate your love for them.

A loving father urges his daughter to release him and
return to life again

A Letter to Aunt Bea

by Glenda Davis

Though I was home by myself that day, I felt someone standing in the doorway right beside me. Yet when I turned to look, no one was there. The feeling stayed with me so strongly that I finally asked out loud, "Who's there?"

Hearing nothing audibly, I began to get clear mental messages. They were emblazoned in white light and consisted of a few words at a time, and they were coming to me from my grandfather. Papa had passed away three days earlier. Across the country, in Alabama, his funeral was just beginning.

"Write to Bea for me," Papa said, speaking of his eldest daughter.

"I don't know what to say to her, Papa," I protested. "I've never written to her before."

Papa assured me that he would tell me exactly what to say, so I finally agreed. Stepping out of the range of my normal, human experience and into another dimension, I was fully aware and functioning in the ordinary physical world. During this time I never felt scared or uneasy at all. We both went into another room that was used as an office, where I sat at the desk to write the letter and Papa sat down near me in the rocking chair.

Beginning the letter with "Dear Aunt Bea," I then waited for direction. The ideas came from my grandfather in blocks of thought, which I translated into my own words. The first thing Papa wanted to tell her was that he was fine and was with Mama, my grandmother who'd passed on three and a half years before.

He went on to say that Aunt Bea's grieving for him was keeping him "earthbound," and he wanted her to let go, release him, and be at peace so that he could move on. It was time for them to say good-bye for now.

When I finished writing all that Papa wanted to say to Bea, he was gone like a poof of smoke.

For fear of being thought strange, I was hesitant to send the letter to Aunt Bea, but I had promised Papa that I would. Since it was a very caring and reassuring letter, I decided to go ahead. Sealing the letter in an envelope, I wrote out the address and sent it.

Aunt Bea wrote back to me, thanking me because the letter had a calming effect on her in such a difficult time. Many years later she still remembered it, saying that it had helped her say farewell to her father and start to heal from the terrible grief she'd suffered after his passing.

Chapter 5

Returning:
A Sacred Promise

It is easy for me to imagine that since the beginning of time those who are intimate with each other have promised to stay connected after death. People sitting under the starry night sky or walking along deserted beaches, lying in front of the fire or sitting by the sickbed through the night have pledged to one another that they would, if possible, return with greetings from the afterlife.

Lovers, brothers, sisters, family, best friends, wives and husbands, parents and children—all who promise each other to return—are vowing to stay connected, to make visible the invisibility of death. It is a vow to reach past the deepest grief and through the seemingly impenetrable veil. This sacred promise carries the hope that we two can be enveloped, for a moment, in the sweet embrace of our special love and can know with certainty that we will be together again.

A promise to return is a mutual acknowledgment that this bond of ours is so essential and important to us, so magnetic, that its pull will be felt even into another realm. Born of love, a powerful intention to make contact may itself create the bridge that enables us to be united consciously, for a moment, though we live in different worlds.

For those who share a special bond, the grief of separation will be a mighty force, a hurricane moving through the heart. The loved one's promise says, I know that you will be in the deep well of grief because when we two must part there will be a rending of the very substance and essence of life. Whoever goes first promises to reach back to assure the other, our parting is temporary, and even when you can't see me, I am here with you always. I promise.

The beautiful selections in this chapter are stories of promises made and fulfilled. A mother is unexpectedly given a promise by her sick child that he will come back to see her after his passing. Best friends agree on the special sign that will be used when one, dying of cancer, reaches the other side. An elderly woman keeps her promise, letting her young cousin know that she is living a splendid life in the hereafter. And finally, a dying mother promises her son that when she returns, it will be clearly and unmistakably her, a sign that he can trust.

Not only do they have one more precious moment together, they are reassured, as we ourselves may be, that shared love and connection continue. The promises say, I love you. Our bond remains strong. I will be here for you when it is your own time to cross over. We will be together again. I know that your heart is grieving, but I am right here, always. Don't worry about me. I am very much alive and very happy!

Fulfilling a vow to return says that not even death can part us; we two live on. That is a sacred promise.

Two hearts are opened to the reality of eternal love

My Heart's Promise

by Gertrud Lorenz

Erica knew the first time that she looked at the little boy that he would die in her arms. Later that afternoon, my sister signed the adoption papers and two-year-old Hans went home with her. It was love at first sight for both of them. Born with a severely damaged heart, Hans was not expected to live to adulthood, and Erica was committed to giving him love and a home until the end, whenever that might come. Their love was one of the most beautiful and intimate that I have ever seen. What they would miss in years they made up for in heart.

Year by year Hans outlived every expectation and grew to be a frail, slender, loving boy with a wonderful mind and a wisdom far beyond his years. In and out of surgery every year or two, he seemed to know from the beginning that he was destined for an abbreviated life. Hans was somehow certain that he would go on to the next life when this one ended. We were not a religious family, so we never really knew where these ideas of an afterlife came from. Feeling that it made the inevitable easier for Hans to deal with, Erica, while not encouraging them, did nothing to dispel them, either.

One day when Hans was eight he walked into his mother's room and gave her his promise that he would come back to see her after he died. Her eyes filled with tears as she was taken aback by his unexpected announcement. To comfort his mother, Hans put his arms around her, saying, "Mummy, everything will be all right." And again he said, "When I go to heaven, I'll come back to see you, I promise."

From that time on, Hans's conversation was sprinkled with references to his promise. "When I die I'll come back and help you in the garden. . . . I promise I'll come home from heaven to take you to the river when the maples turn red. . . . Mummy, I'll come back for Christmas. I promise. When I'm in heaven . . ."

Even though Erica knew from the beginning that Hans would not live a long life, still she dreaded the day of its completion. That day came when Hans was ten. Only a week after his last surgery, Hans died peacefully in Erica's arms. His damaged heart was beyond further repair. My sister, inconsolable for a time, took leave from her post as pediatrician at the community health clinic to rest and grieve her loss. Deeply grateful for the years they'd had together, Erica knew that she had been able to provide Hans with a full life, and she was certain that he knew love while he lived.

She was not religious, and as much as she longed to see her son, she held, sadly, that life was not this way. That is why I was so surprised, shocked really, when, about two years after Hans had died, Erica told me that he came to her in a dream. She said, "It was not like an ordinary dream at all. It was beyond description. It was . . ." She was at a loss for words. "I felt more awake than I have ever been in my life. It was like magic." Hans wanted to show her that he is alive. "And, Gertrud," she said to me, "he looked wonderful. He wasn't sick anymore. He was a healthy teenager!" Her eyes danced with joy, even as she wondered aloud, "Maybe I'm crazy, but I think it really happened!"

Changed after her dream, Erica seemed happy, like someone with a wonderful secret. Although in some way she still questioned her sanity because of the experience, she was unable to deny how much it had opened her heart and filled her with joy.

A few months later, Erica came to Christmas dinner at our home. We were alone in the kitchen preparing the meal when she told me that Hans had come to her again, this time while she was wide awake. Her eyes were so radiant as she spoke about the experience that I felt my own eyes well up with emotion. The intensity and depth of her emotion went through me also, and we ended up both in tears, in a deep embrace. As the children and my husband came through the kitchen door, Erica winked at me, saying, "I haven't told you the most important part. I will tell you everything tomorrow."

Erica stayed at our house that night. We all went to bed around ten, and my sister never woke up. She suffered a brain aneurysm sometime during the night, according to the doctors, and died instantly.

My own heart was opened by my sister's death. That Hans did come to Erica, I have no doubt. I believe that he promised to be there for her when it was time for her passage into the next life, just as Erica was always there for him in this world.

The promise to meet again brings two friends back together

Face-to-Face

by Dixie Gamble

I hate cell phones. They're unhealthy, unholy, and unwise. But tonight, Christmas Eve, as we slowly snake our way down the congested, smog-enshrouded L.A. freeway, this baneful phone is a lifeline. On the other end, most of a continent away in Nashville, my comatose friend, Dale, is dying. A hospital phone is held up next to her ear, and I say my farewell and carry out one of our prearranged death agreements: when she was ready to leave I would assist her crossing.

Prayerfully, I fumble for the right words to support my friend of twenty years in loosening her grasp on the rim of life. "You can do it, Dale, it's exactly like we talked about, just let go and leap." Suddenly my words sound hollow, banal; we're talking about death here, quitting life, not quitting a job or leaving a relationship. This isn't even a life-or-death decision. It's a face-to-face, toe-to-toe leap into life's greatest fear. I am rocked by a wave of that fear as it crashes through the phone line. Is this Dale's fear or mine? The urgency of her struggle with letting go of all she knows for some great unknown penetrates my gut like surges of electric shock. For an instant I glimpse the freedom that awaits her, then wince as freedom spins into panic.

Confusion is palpable as my friend desperately grips the edges of the earth, knuckles turning white, stiffening fingers tiring, struggling to hold on and struggling also to let go. Tears pound out a rhythm on my breast, soaking the soft cashmere of my Christmas Eve dress.

Holding my breath, I am suddenly reminded of birthing my sons, how the moment of deepest pain drew me to hold my breath and push. Yes! This is it! Dale is making her way down the birth canal, and I'm her midwife to another life. "Dale, push! Push yourself out of your body, you can do it!"

All at once, memory takes me back to that bright October day when, christening our last time spent together, the sun breathed prisms of rainbow light through the leaded windows. We snuggled warmly around each other in front of the open fire. I stared at Dale too long and too much, not wanting to pull my gaze from her face for fear of forgetting every lovely nuance. "Now," she began matter-of-factly, as if addressing her board of directors. "I want you to help me die, if that becomes necessary. I mean, if I chicken out or anything, remind me that I'm not afraid. I'm not afraid of death, but who knows how I'll react when dying becomes the only choice I have in the moment. I don't want to go over carrying a carload of fear with me."

I nod in agreement, a weak smile joining my cascading tears. "And, Dixie," Dale went on, "we need to be able to know conclusively if, indeed, I can consciously reach you and you can consciously know that it's me. I mean, beyond any shadow of doubt. How can we do that?"

"It has to be tangible," I said, "beyond doubt. I've got an idea. Why don't you touch my cheek with an eagle feather, and I'll definitely know it's you. Nobody but you would do that."

"Perfect," she purred, flashing her toothy smile, the one that always held her entire face captive. "When you feel the feather drawn across your cheek, stop and breathe deeply so you'll be open to me."

When I left that day, it did not occur to me that it would be the last time I saw my friend's wonderful, familiar face.

An earthly jolt of reality brings me out of remembering and back into the car, back to Christmas Eve. We've arrived at the church, and my husband John's family will be inside, lifting their voices in celebration of a holy child's birth.

I wonder if my words are reaching her through the labyrinth of my rising emotion, and I feel as if I'm moving through molasses, knowing that my link to Dale will soon be disconnected. Hanging up that phone is one of the hardest things I've ever had to do. "I understand, Dale, I understand, my friend, how hard it is to let go."

A little later, sitting numbly on the hard church pew, vaguely aware of the church choir singing, "Silent night, holy night, all is calm, all is bright," suddenly I know—Dale's gone home.

Christmas Day I fly to Nashville and go immediately to Dale's humble palace, which had once been a barn. Much has been left undone. Death is a work in progress. There are presents undelivered, cards not sent, lists unchecked. The ubiquitous spirit of the barn house has departed. Shivering at the inert emptiness, I invite the dogs inside to keep me company. Their sad, moist eyes mourn the loss of their beloved keeper.

I am kept busy for three days. On that third and final night, exhausted from the weight of grief, the unending list of to-do's, and my overwhelming sense of responsibility to get it all done, I crash into bed before ten o'clock. Somewhere in the night, I'm abruptly awakened by Dale's dogs barking excitedly. Their voices are insistent. Am I in danger, is this a warning?

My heart rolls in my chest, pounding adrenaline through my body. Somebody's in the house! Everybody knew about Dale's death; her obituary was front-page news. She was the road manager for the Grateful Dead for many years; then, as founder of Leadership Music, she was a mover and shaker in the music community of Nashville, widely known and loved. Now her house is being robbed, with me in it!

Frightened beyond fear, I freeze, my face to the wall. Holding my breath to erase my presence, I don't move a muscle. Seconds later someone is in the room, standing by my bed. Don't move, just don't move, and they'll go away.

Someone leans over me, brushing my cheek with all the softness of heaven, all the softness of an eagle's feather. "It's Dale." Her voice falls sweet and clear into my ear.

My response startled me then and still does to this day. I am terrified. After all we'd plotted and planned, I am completely and utterly terrified. My face is still to the wall while Dale slips into bed beside me, spooning her being around my body.

"It's really you! Dale! You did it!" My words pour out in a torrent of excitement tinged with fear. I am chagrined about my fear and hope Dale doesn't notice.

"It's terribly difficult for me to be here, Dixie, but I wanted to come. I promised. I wanted to show you that I could."

I'm mortified that here I am, actually carrying on a conversation with a someone from the other side, and I'm unable to think of one universal question. I ask her, "What's it like? Is it everything we believed it would be?"

"Everything and more. It's everything all at once." Dale's voice sounds resonant and present. I feel her body shift on the bed beside me. "I can't stay long," she adds. "I don't have the power yet."

"What do you mean?" I stammer for words. "There's so much I want to know."

"I'm new to this form," she says. "It's hard to keep my energy focused."

More than anything in that electric moment, I want to see her face. But I am too frightened to turn over to look at her. Did I suppose I'd see some chilling ghostly apparition? I don't know. What I do know is that, lying beside me, Dale exudes wholeness, completeness, love without borders, life plugged into its perpetual source.

With crystalline clarity, I can feel that she wears the cloak of eternity while retaining her bodily characteristics and personality. Her scent is the pure essence of Dale. Her hair the same silky texture, her voice the same unique rasp. Every quality I knew to be Dale seems omnipresent in the moment.

I feel the bed move as she rises to leave. "I'm going now."

Summoning all of my courage, I roll over to see her face one last time. I am stunned into wonder and reverence as I see that her image is clear, intact, though somewhat different. Her arms, floating at her sides, seem long in proportion to the rest of her ethereal body, which is small, somewhat translucent, and ambiguously formed. Her legs seem weak, undeveloped. Her movement is unsure, unsteady, like an infant in development, learning how to manage her body. That's it!

In that moment Dale's parting gift wrapped itself around my being, bringing me to my knees in awe. A newborn! Birth and death are one and the same. One no more powerful or frightening than the other, both are simply an ordained part of the endless cycle. I watch as Dale vanishes through the wall of her beloved barn home, without emotional attachment or hesitation.

She was on a mission, to grow strong in her new existence, just as she had been strong in her earthly life. This earthly plane of life had no pull for her now. She was simply and lovingly fulfilling her promise.

"Goodbye, Dale." My lips formed the words that filled the empty room. My heart held the love that filled the vacant space in my life.

As promised, a mother's timely message for her son

A Promise in Time
by Fred Leyda

Kind of a foolish thing to worry about when your mom is dying, but I was worried that from the afterlife she would find out everything—all the little and not-so-little things I'd done that I wasn't really proud of.

"I'll love you no matter what," she lovingly reassured me. "Fred, you're always trying to be what everyone *else* wants you to be. Why don't you just *be yourself!*"

As we talked more about her impending death, I asked her to promise that, one way or another, she'd come back and let me know if she is alive and happy and if all that we believed about the afterlife was true.

I wanted her to contact me in some way that would be unmistakable to me, something that would leave no doubt in my mind. Not when I was asleep, not in a dream, not through any kind of cryptic events, no! I wanted her to promise that she'd come back in the middle of the day, when I was wide awake and could make sure there was no confusion. Mom promised she would do her best.

After Mother died I strongly felt her presence all around me. Later that week, as my father and I sorted through her things, I told him about Mom's promise and about my feelings that she was still close by, still with me.

"Well," he said, "if your mother really is contacting you, you'll know from this clock." My father looked at me knowingly as he handed me the clock, which had been on our mantle while I was growing up. At the time I never asked what he meant by that or why he'd said it. I merely took the clock back to my own home, something special by which to remember Mom.

Two weeks after Mom's death, when I was back at home in Florida, I received a call from my friend Kim. Though we had lived together years earlier, we'd been completely out of touch for a number of years. Kim said that for two weeks she'd been trying to find me. I'd moved so many times it wasn't easy, but she said she felt driven to find me.

Kim told me that she'd been feeling an overwhelming need to tell me something. She said, "I have the feeling that you're about to do something really serious in your life, and I have to tell you, *don't do it!*"

Now she didn't know it at the time, but I was engaged to be married. When I told her about my plans, she immediately began shouting that my mother was there. "It's her! It's her! It's your mom, and she wants me to tell you not to get married!"

I explained that it wouldn't be very polite to tell my fiancée that I can't marry her because my dead mother visited an old friend and told her to tell me not to do it. But Kim just kept insisting that I couldn't, I mustn't, go through with the wedding.

Finally we changed the subject and began catching up on what had been happening in our lives. As we were talking, I mentally asked, "Mom, is this really you? Are you really there with Kim?" I didn't say anything out loud but only thought it in my mind.

As I asked that question, immediately I felt an electric charge run down the right side of my body, like a million ants crawling over me, and the very next words out of my friend's mouth had nothing to do with our conversation. Out of the blue Kim said, "You're always trying to be what everyone *else* wants you to be. Why don't you just *be yourself!*"

Of course I was surprised. Kim had repeated my mom's last words verbatim, and not even in the context of the conversation we were having. They came out of nowhere.

Our amazing conversation continued. I was so excited that, phone in hand, I was pacing all over my apartment. As we were getting ready to hang up, once again I mentally asked, "Please, Mom, if this is really you, I need another sign, to be absolutely sure."

At that instant and, again, out of context, my friend says, "Your mom is here, and she is saying to tell you, yes, things are the way you believe, she is happy where she is and not to grieve about her death. She says that your dad will have a rough time for a little while, but he'll be okay. And your mother says for you to right now, immediately, look over your right shoulder!"

I instantly turned and looked over my right shoulder, and there, right in front of my face, was the clock that had been on the mantle in my childhood home. The same clock that my father had given me with the words, "If it's really your mother, you'll know from this clock."

I had been pacing all over my apartment, so there was no way anyone could have known where I was standing, let alone which direction I was facing. Not to mention the fact that my friend was calling me from over two thousand miles away.

From that day on, I have absolutely no doubt that my mother is alive and happy and that there is an afterlife where I will see her again. My mom kept her promise to contact me from the other side in a way that would be unmistakable to me.

By the way, Mom was right. I found out about a month before the wedding that my fiancée had been cheating on me the entire time we were engaged. I called off the wedding and didn't even have to blame it on my mother.

This visitation did much to soothe the grief of losing my mother, and it assured me not only that we will be together again but also that she knows and cares about what is going on in my life.

The individuality and vitality of life continue

The Divine Fern
by Shirley Hocking

My dear cousin Fern was quite tall and gangly, loved to wear red, and took dancing lessons to be more graceful. She kept a daily log on scraps of old paper, junk mail, old labels, and whatever. Marjorie Fern Smith was her name, and she was my mother's first cousin.

Fern had had three husbands and told me once that all of them were "top drawer people." She always said that her first husband was just plain wild sex, the second was more romance, and the third husband was for security.

As a memento from her first marriage, Fern had saved a sterling silver spoon, which she used at breakfast every morning because it reminded her of the great passion of that time and allowed her to "start the day on a high note."

Cousin Fern died the day after her ninety-fourth birthday. Many of her husbands' and boyfriends' families attended her funeral, with lots of wonderful stories of her very active love life. Once, shortly before her passing, I asked Fern how she was planning to handle the inevitable encounters with her three former husbands and all of her many, many lovers once she got to heaven. Her snappy reply was, "Well, that won't be a problem. I'll just wear a red dress and red lingerie."

Looking forward to death as her "graduation," Fern promised me that she would keep in touch with me after she died, to assure me that she was all right and let me know how she was doing in her new life. It was a wonderful comfort to me when, about a month after her death, she did indeed pay me a visit.

Cousin Fern was wearing a beautiful, bright red party dress. She told me that she and her mother, who had died about twenty years earlier, were living together in a wonderful apartment. As promised, Fern came back to assure me that she was very, very well indeed.

The second visitation came about a month later. Again wearing her red party dress, the dancing Fern was jumping around the room and clicking her heels with joy as she told me not to grieve for her, that she was very happy in the new life and having a grand time.

I don't doubt it for a minute.

Chapter 6

Life After:
Visions of the Afterlife

The afterlife, heaven, the great beyond, the hereafter, nirvana, the next world, the other side—the greatest of all mysteries is called by myriad names. People have always wondered what the afterlife is like. Do people remain individuals with their own personalities? Do they have bodies? What do they do there? Can they see me? Reflecting more than mere curiosity, the questions are endless.

Every visitation, regardless of its message, reveals a great deal of information. If anyone can communicate with us from the afterlife in any way at all, it shows that life after death is a reality, that a significant degree of individuality is retained, and that our connection continues and can cross the apparent barriers that separate us.

Some visitations specifically and intentionally go further into the mystery of the hereafter, giving us evocative hints, glimpses into life on the other side. These visitations bring greatly needed comfort and healing to those who, immersed in grief, are finding it impossible to heal without knowing where and how their loved one is living. It is impossible for our hearts and minds to imagine that our beloved is nowhere and nonexistent; to find peace we must be able to place them somewhere. We are given a symbolic image of the vast, multidimensional reality of the afterlife, translated for us into a human understanding of place so that we can begin to heal.

A powerful aspect of unrelenting grief for some people can be the deep, sometimes urgent, need to know not only if their loved one is alive but also if he or she is all right, whole once again after an accident or debilitating illness. Has his suffering ended? Is she alone or being cared for by friends and family? Does he miss me? Is she afraid? These are not questions of the intellect. Asked in the depths of the heart, such questions may haunt our sleepless nights and fill our very dreams.

Even a small glimpse into the new life may be enough to return us to some measure of peace by giving the needed reassurance of continued life and restored health and wholeness. We see and feel for ourselves that our loved one is well cared for and dwells in happiness.

Through numerous visitation accounts, many small pieces of a vast picture emerge. Though we are never able to see the whole picture, piece after piece suggests that the afterlife is not a place per se; rather, it seems to be a state of consciousness, a reflection of each individual's deepest soul needs at the time of death. If rest is needed, some time may be spent in a peaceful place of recuperation. Another person in need of care may be surrounded by old friends and family. Seeking spiritual understanding, guidance, and insight might be the greatest imperative for yet another. Individuality and personality are retained into the next life, with occasional expressions of the old, very earthly sense of humor.

Great freedom of movement exists, along with unlimited creative possibilities. In an unobstructed universe without time or space as we know them, thought immediately draws to you that which you imagine and hold in consciousness. Imagine a particular person or place, and you are there!

People commonly appear in visitations to be between twenty-five and thirty-five years old, radiantly youthful and beautiful, extraordinarily whole and healthy even if death occurred at the age of ninety-seven or because of a ravaging illness. The spiritual body apparently retains many of its previous characteristics though few of its previous limitations.

And of dying itself, those who speak of it frequently say that it was not painful or difficult. They tell of gently, gently slipping out of the physical body and into the light. More than once I have heard that an individual was completely unaware of her own passing out of the body until she happened to hear others in the room speaking of it. Only then did she realize that the transition had already occurred with the painless ease of a fragrance drifting out of a just-opened perfume bottle.

From many accounts of visitations and near-death experiences, there emerges a picture of a dimension in which life is so beautiful and rich that it seems almost too wonderful to be true, a heavenly magic kingdom where all the rides are free. We hear of unlimited creativity, perfect harmony, unimaginable beauty, and the pervasive atmosphere of love and oneness with everything. Perhaps our ancient images of paradise are based on the reality of life in the hereafter.

The afterlife is a realm of transformation—of body, mind, and spirit—a place lovingly reflecting the consciousness of each individual and his or her place in the great cosmic dance of eternity.

The great mystery of the world beyond will, of course, remain a mystery until the time of our own journey there. Until that time, and may it be a long, long time from now, visitation stories provide evocative fragments to fire the imagination and soothe our grieving hearts.

One man's perspective on the moments just after death

In Prayer and Singing
by Carol Gottesman

Ernie was a cantor, one who leads the congregation in prayer and singing. I sensed that Ernie was close by all day following his death, and later that afternoon I knew that my beloved husband was present right there with me. Speaking to me in my mind and heart, he told me that he would never leave me, "for we are together for eternity." We would now, he told me, be learning to grow on a whole new level.

"Ernie," I asked, "what was it like when you died? Did you feel pain? Are you in the presence of angels?"

"No, I didn't feel any pain," he assured me. "I just felt myself being very gently pulled out of my body and then found that I was in a loving presence.

"I didn't even realize that I had died until I heard the nurses saying that I was gone. Then I thought of you, and instantly I was there with you. My next thought was of my daughter, and instantly I found myself there with her." Ernie quickly realized that all he had to do was think of something and it happened immediately.

He said that he was with me when I left the house and went to the nursing home. "You helped me so much," he said, "because you were so calm. You didn't say that you had to say good-bye to *me*, you said you had to say good-bye to the body. So when you left I went with you." He was even able to be with a number of loved ones as they heard the sad news of his passing.

Freedom from the encumbrances of his ill body left him joyous, a newborn learning to navigate in a new body.

Ernie's presence stayed with me throughout my long period of intense anguish and grieving, comforting me and supporting me when I needed him the most. Now, four years later, he is with me still, embracing me like the warmth of the sun. He continues to teach me that, although the body dies, the essence or spirit continues. Growth and learning and life continue.

I know that love is eternal. Not even death can part us.

Revealing a realm of personal fulfillment and creativity

Father's First Return

by Lee Lawson

Alone in the house late in the afternoon, sitting on my bed, I was just about to start my eleventh-grade homework when suddenly the room was filled with a shimmering, glowing light. The light was unmistakably Father, as clearly as though I could see his face.

Just a second later, when he communicated to me internally to close my eyes, I immediately found myself standing next to him. I was filled with joy that no words could describe. He had died two months earlier, after almost two years of being ravaged by cancer, chemotherapy, and radiation treatments.

Father then spoke, saying, "I know how deeply disturbed you were seeing me suffer so much, and I know that it is still with you. I want you to see me and see for yourself that I am not suffering anymore. I want you to know that I am happy, and I want you to see where I live now."

Then, taking a long, clear look at him, I saw that my father was radiant with health, appearing healthier than healthy. Young and handsome, he was bursting with energy and vitality. Father drew my attention to a T-shirt that he was wearing. Emblazoned across the front, it read, "Hale, Hearty, and Full of Life!" Father then motioned that he wanted me to follow him so that he could show me where he lived. Coming to a place outside, where there were many, many people engaged in a great variety of activities, Father said that here people spend their time doing what they love to do. We passed by people playing music, painting at easels, sculpting, riding horses, and a thousand other things. Happiness radiated from every face. I didn't really hear music; I felt it. It might sound a bit like a heavenly summer camp, but that is what I saw.

After a time we returned to the place where we'd started, and it was clearly time to part. My father spoke to me of some deeply meaningful personal things and told me some of what would occur in our family in the future. We said good-bye.

That day, the extreme anguish and distress I'd felt at seeing my young father suffer so horribly before his death was eased with the knowledge that he was living in a place of great personal fulfillment and radiant health. His suffering had been wiped away, leaving not a trace. I knew this in my heart, for I had been taken there myself for a moment. Being totally immersed in its atmosphere permeated with tangible, palpable love and joy, I saw and felt for myself his peace, serenity, and wholeness. Not only was he whole in body, he was whole in mind and spirit as well. And I could begin to heal.

Once again I was aware of sitting on my bed, homework in front of me, tears running down my cheeks.

Wisdom from another point of view

We-Body

by Talasteena

Eighty-nine years strong, my father, Samuel Kern, born in Vienna, was a Holocaust survivor. Uneducated, he completed only the first few grades of primary school in Europe before beginning his career as a milliner.

At the time of his death he didn't believe in God, though he suspected that maybe there was a place one goes after death. He was uncertain whether death was final, and when, about a month before he died, we discussed the possibility of life after death, he hesitatingly agreed to communicate with me if he could.

Twelve hours after his passing, around 3 A.M., I was awakened from deep sleep, jolted into an upright position, alert and surprised as I heard the words "Hi, Dad" emanating from my own lips. My father was present in the room and wanted to talk. Without another thought or judgment I grabbed my bedside journal and began to write down all that Dad was saying to me.

"It begins almost at once," he told me, "dying. Yesterday, I left my body behind. What was it like? Just as there are many kernels on a cob of corn, you eat some, some remain. You eat a few more, fewer remain until all are ingested. That's what it was like, leaving my body, bit by bit, until I was there no more. It was easy to say good-bye.

"Even though the spirit doesn't entirely disconnect from the body, that's what it felt like as I loosened and streamed out. I felt my spirit immediately begin to move toward the Source. You knew all along what I wanted there toward the end of my life, to reconnect with all that is peaceful and wise. I missed the feeling of wisdom. It waits for me now."

In speaking with me about a particular situation in my life, Dad said, "Part of why it is difficult for you is that you think of yourself as you—body, somebody, nobody, anybody—when you really are a *we-body*. I have fewer thoughts for you as a separate being now."

Of his new state, Dad said, "There is an intelligence so grand and so intricate and so minute you couldn't imagine, a largeness, a vastness, and I am still only a part of the part, so my knowing doesn't yet include all, but all includes mine already."

In the course of this time together, my father and I talked of many things, both personal family things and things of the soul. Dad's words to me not only satisfied my questions about life after death, they also helped me over the deep grief of his passing. Seeing my life a part of the larger design of creation encouraged me to let go and move on to a more soul-satisfying life.

The blessing of his presence and his words fills me to this day and has transformed my life from the inside out.

For rest and recovery

A Place Apart

by Neil Tessler

She was an avid reader of pulp fiction. Our bookshelves held a wide collection of novels of the type commonly found at the supermarket checkout. My mother was a vital and intelligent individual though quite attached to her creature comforts and upper-middle-class suburban lifestyle. I might add that my mother was an absolute atheist who never gave a serious thought in her life to spiritual issues regarding this world or the next.

After a ten-year struggling with cancer, Mother died from the complications of chemotherapy. Because of my own professional involvement with complementary medicine, I was distressed during those years that she had no interest in trying alternatives to standard treatment. Finally, after a period of grieving, I accepted that it was her life and her death and that my mother had the right to choose to live and die according to her own nature.

A few hours after Mother's last breath, exhausted but at peace, I lay down to take some needed rest. In a matter of moments I saw my mother right there before me. She was lovely and appeared fifteen years younger, completely free of the chronic Bell's palsy that had taken away her looks many years before. Mother had a radiant, exuberant smile on her face. Behind her was the place where she now was to stay.

Mother showed me that she would live for a time in a one-room cabin in a healing pastoral, country setting. Inside, her room contained a simple bed and bookshelves. Everything appeared to be made of plain, unvarnished wood. Books of spiritual literature filled the shelf. Mother was alone there, a condition of life she had never known when alive.

I was immediately struck by the total contradiction of this environment with the world in which she had lived while on earth, and I knew it was a place Mother never would have chosen consciously while she was alive. Yet it was now her place to rest, to heal, and to divest herself of the materialistic values that had so firmly dominated her earthly life.

The next day at the funeral, my father, with tears filling his eyes, revealed that he, too, had seen my mother. She had appeared to him as she had appeared to me while he dozed in a chair at about the same time I was lying down.

He exclaimed that she had appeared as real as I was, now sitting beside him. Bending down to kiss him, Mother lovingly said, "I want you to be happy now."

I believe that both my father and I were able to be much more at peace regarding Mother's very long and difficult illness and passing knowing that she was in a place of rest and recuperation, partaking of the deepest healing and rebalancing of body, mind, and spirit.

Though she appeared as a young woman, he recognized
his grandmother's essence

On the Beach
by Karl Michel

As I stood on the beach in Malibu looking out at the Pacific Ocean, my beloved grandmother came out of the water, through the breaking surf, and sat down on a rock just a few feet in front of me.

My grandmother and I had been very close. She lived with my family while I was growing up, and we were together much of the time. A short while before she died, she had made some medical choices regarding treatment and was very clear about the consequences of her decisions. Her only regret was that I was leaving, moving to California, and wouldn't be there with her when she died. Although it was very painful for me, I could not postpone my departure. Grandmother died two months after I left.

Now, on the beach, Grandmother appeared to be a glorious young woman in her twenties, although the last time we had been together she had been an elderly and quite sick woman of ninety-one. Now she was in radiant good health, wearing Capri pants and a sleeveless top. I recognized her immediately, not by her physical appearance, since I do not recall ever seeing her that age, but by her essence. I can't really explain it. I just knew.

"Grandmother, what is it like to be dead?" I asked. "Is it like dreaming?"

"You would like to think that," she replied enigmatically, and I knew then that she was not able to answer my question directly. I had the immediate realization and understanding that infinitely more important than our trying to communicate through words was the very fact of our being there together. Grandmother and I spent several moments in wordless communion until, finally, she slipped back into the water and disappeared from view.

On the beach together, Grandmother revealed to me beyond any doubt that our bond of love transcended death and that she was well. Not only was she well, she was young and radiant and seemingly more alive and profoundly whole than ever. Curious about the fact that she looked so young, I wondered if there was a reversal of the aging process in the afterlife. Her youth and radiantly healthy appearance said more to me about the afterlife than could ever be said in words.

I was tremendously comforted by my grandmother's visitation on the beach. It gave me the certainty of knowing that she is deeply happy in the next world.

Walking into another realm, a scholar experiences for himself the reality of the afterlife

A Beautiful View

by Leon Rhodes

I was alone in the house that afternoon. As I stood in front of the fireplace, leaning on the mantel, quite unexpectedly the fire, the fireplace, and the mantel simply dissolved away, opening up a strikingly beautiful vista, and I was able to walk directly into it. As I entered this realm, there was my father, who had died many years earlier. I was greatly comforted to see that though he'd been in frail and failing health the last time I'd seen him, now he looked fully whole and healthy.

"Those times we used to talk about the spiritual world and the life awaiting us all," he said, "you should know that it is all quite true!" My father revealed to me that once in the afterlife, we do indeed join those beloved friends and family members with whom we share similar values and ideas. Each of us being different, we find our experience in the afterlife is a clear reflection of who and what we hold in consciousness.

My father made known to me that the joys of heaven are indescribable and never ending, being of beauty and harmony barely conceivable through the human mind, a paradise. After he conveyed to me the reality of the afterlife, my father slowly began to fade away. Once more aware of the mantelpiece and fireplace, I found myself back in our living room. I believe that I stood there for a while before sitting down in my usual easy chair.

For more than twenty years, as a teacher and lecturer on the subject of near-death experiences (NDEs), I have thought much about the relationship between the spiritual world and those of us still living on earth, but I don't recall that this was on my mind that day as I stood next to the fireplace and found myself in another world. After my vision I sensed that now, because I had actually experienced being conscious in another realm and had spoken with my father, I was finally really able to write and lecture about the NDE without the subconscious doubt and uncertainty I had sometimes felt.

My father's visit has stayed in my memory in such a way that whenever I speak or write about the afterlife, I have a tangible sense of his assurance, and it bolsters my confidence, making it much easier to convey my message of continued life and reunion with those we love.

Reassuring us all that our individuality and sense of humor follow us into the hereafter

Baloney!

by Paula Peterson

My friend was disturbingly distraught. Never before had I witnessed someone who grieved so deeply over the death of a parent. Yet there was not much I could do to ease his anguish and suffering.

During the funeral service, as we listened to various speakers give their eulogies, I caught a wispy glimpse of my friend's dead father standing in front of the audience with a big smile on his face, beaming with pride and appreciation, obviously enthralled with the crowd that had gathered to see him off.

Again and again I caught glimpses of him making amusing gestures, responding differently as each speaker told of the times they had spent together with him while he was alive. At one point, a particular minister got up and spewed forth an overly flowery account of the dead man. Much to my surprise, I saw the departed father theatrically pinch his nose to communicate that the minister's speech stank. "Full of baloney!" he cried out, emphatically waving his arms in the air.

After the service I cautiously shared with my grieving friend all that I'd seen and heard. Even though I worried at first that it might upset him even more, I told him what I'd seen his father doing during the memorial. My friend did not get upset; on the contrary, he heartily and joyfully embraced my report of his father's reaction to the minister's eulogy, saying that his father often made exactly the same theatrical gesture, pinching his nose and waving his arms at people and events that he thought not true. "Full of baloney!" he would always say. And my friend had to agree that the minister had embellished things quite a bit in his praise.

Sharing my vision gave my friend the comfort and peace of mind he needed to know that his father was not only alive and well in his life after death but also still wonderfully himself, full of all his old mischief!

Chapter 7

Touch:
Touching and Being Touched

One of my favorite stories about grief is the story of a Zen master whose beloved teacher dies. The master, beside himself with grief, is wailing inconsolably. He is in agony, tears flooding from his eyes. His followers come into the room saying, "Master, why are you so distraught? You of all people know that there is no death! The people outside—what will they think, hearing you, the master, wailing like this?" The master looks up through his sobs and replies, "Yes, indeed, I know there is no death, but," he says, holding out his trembling hands, "tell that to these hands, which will never touch that beloved face again."

Of all of our sensory expressions, touch is the most intimate. Touch is what we share with others, the most personal meeting reserved for a few special people in our lives. Being touched during a visitation is just as real as being touched in ordinary life. A physical, visceral, emotional response remains even after the touch has ended. The unmistakable pressure of an embrace is felt by the body as well as by the heart and soul.

In this chapter I have gathered stories in which touch is central to the message of comfort and love. In the first five stories, powerful and vivid experiences of touching and embrace are at the heart of the encounter, giving an undeniable reality and immediacy to the moment. The touch is visceral, tangible, and three-dimensional, anything but ethereal. It is warm and alive and is received as the unique and loving touch of a particular beloved individual.

There has always been mystery surrounding the occurrence of touch in a visitation from the afterlife. It is far less commonly experienced than visual and auditory communication; perhaps it is more difficult to accomplish from the spirit world. When it does occur, touch brings profound comfort and incredible joy because it is so undeniable. The mind can disbelieve sight and sound, but touch, as it reverberates throughout your being, is harder to dismiss as simply fantasy or wishful thinking. It is very hard to conjure up a convincing bear hug.

Another aspect of touch during visitations is fascinating. Over the years I have been told many stories of reunions in which someone, while reaching out to embrace a departed loved one, was lovingly but firmly implored, "Don't touch me!" Many people will recall that Jesus said these words to Mary Magdalene when he appeared to her after the resurrection. The request not to touch comes up over and over in stories of visitations, and we can only wonder why it is that so often we are directed, in no uncertain terms, not to make physical contact.

Some people, understandably unable to resist the powerful and perhaps overwhelming desire to embrace a loved one, reach out anyway, only to find themselves quite suddenly alone. The last two stories in this selection on touch give vivid examples of this mysterious, emphatic injunction, "Don't touch me!"

Some things can never be forgotten

My Mother's Touch

by Mary Ann Jordan

Mother was my best friend. Even though I was a grown woman with two small children, we were inseparable. She taught me to cook and was always there to give me advice and help with my children. I felt so blessed to be able to move back home to live with her after my marriage ended in divorce.

When my mother died of cancer at the age of fifty-two, I felt that my life had ended as well. Feeling completely alone, I was so devastated that I would actually pray, begging God to send my mother back to me. Deeply enshrouded in grief, I was barely able to work or care for my children. I was sinking deeper and deeper into despair.

"Wake up, Mary." I was awakened from sleep by the touch of Mother's warm hand on my arm. Opening my eyes, I saw her sitting there next to me, smiling down at me. Always a beautiful woman, my mother now looked even more radiantly beautiful than ever before. She glowed with peace and light. No pain was on her face, as when I last saw her.

Still touching my arm, she said simply, "Mary, you have got to stop grieving for me and go on with your life. Make a life for yourself and for those babies. Raise them the way I taught you. Give them plenty of love. It won't be long before we are all together again. Promise me now that you will stop this grieving."

I promised my mother that I would try. Gently touching each of my sleeping children on their heads, my mother turned back to me, and with love filling her eyes, she said, "Mary, I must go now." She disappeared quietly, and I was left there in the room with my two sleeping children.

After that I was able to go on with my life, able to take care of my children and our home. I have tried not to grieve over her anymore. But it has been twenty-eight years since she died, and I still miss her deeply every day of my life.

Although some of my friends who know about this claim I was probably dreaming, I know that isn't true. My mother touched me, and you never forget your mother's touch.

Following a beautiful symbolic message, her father's unmistakable touch
comes at the moment of her greatest despair

The Land of the Long White Cloud
by Alwyn Lewis

My story has its beginning in the part of New Zealand known as the Land of the Long White Cloud. This is a land rich in mythology. Legend has it that the great God Maui, while out in his canoe fishing one day, snared a very big fish. He pulled and pulled on his line and to his amazement pulled in, not the huge fish he expected, but New Zealand's South Island. This is a land where Gods are all-powerful and the land happily reflects this power.

My father was born in 1904 when New Zealand was in its infancy. His parents were first-generation New Zealanders of Scottish parentage, and at his birth he was baptized and given the name Huia, a Maori name, given by the Maori woman who conducted the ceremony. The Huia, a beautiful native bird, now extinct, was sacred to the Maori people.

At the time of my father's death, the sorrow I felt was profound. We flew with our family from Australia to be present at the funeral service and stayed in his house. That night as I lay in bed, thinking back over the events of the day, the morepork, a small owl, called three times. I knew in my heart that it held great meaning for us.

Over the following days as we sorted out belongings in the house, the morepork's call stayed in the front of my consciousness. Telling myself I was overreacting from grief, that I was tired and not thinking straight, did nothing to dispel the belief that the bird's call was for a reason.

The day before we were to leave New Zealand to return to our home in Australia, I noticed Sir Ralph Love, a Maori elder, family friend, and deeply respected leader of the Maori people, cutting flax in his driveway across the road from my father's house.

"I want to ask you about the morepork's call." My words tumbled out.

He looked at me intently for a moment, then at the ground. "What about the morepork?"

"Do the Maoris hear the morepork call?"

"Perhaps," he replied.

"I heard it. It called three times. I had the definite feeling it was trying to say something."

He looked at me again then slowly, as he always did, put his arm around my shoulder, saying, "Then I will tell you. Of course, my dear. Of course. All things are connected. The morepork's call was telling you your father had reached the other place."

Later that day as the plane took off from Wellington airport and headed south over the snowcapped peaks, the morepork's call stayed with me. Throughout the flight I felt myself becoming overwhelmed by increasing feelings of grief and anguish. Just when the feeling was at its unbearable peak, my father's strong hands reached over the seat from behind and steadied my shoulders. I not only felt them, I saw them! In that moment I had the joyous knowledge that there was no separation and that everything was in its place and exactly as it should be.

In the nine years since my father's caress steadied me and carried me through my darkest moment, all that I experienced has remained intact and clear. I can still feel the warmth and pressure of his loving hands on my shoulders, and I can hear the morepork's call telling me Father reached "the other place." Time and space seem measures that apply only to us here.

This experience after his death has given me renewed hope of a meeting with loved ones again and has reassured me that this life is simply a stepping-off place into the infinite.

*Healing assurance that love transcends time and space
and lives in eternity*

A Love Story Without End

by Barbara Duncan

This is a love story. It has no beginning and no end.

Often in my adult life, I had prayed a desperate prayer, "Please, God, don't let me die without knowing what it's like to love and really be loved in return!" I had just about conceded the fact that perhaps this was not to be, and I contented myself with the love of family, children, and grandchildren.

Then along came Leroy and five and a half years of the most incredible love and happiness. He had prayed that same prayer. Our love was beyond anything I had ever imagined. It was if we had always been together. When we talked about the past we each said "in my other life," for within our relationship there was the freedom to be and become what we had only dared to dream of before.

Leroy retired early, only two years into our time together. We purchased an RV, called it our "little house," and launched ourselves into the wonderful world of travel.

We relished those times to the point of selfishness. We invited no one to travel or stay with us in our little house. We were snowbirds in the winter and traveled extensively in the summer. After three years of traveling in this way, we were toying with the idea of locking up the house for a year and just roaming around the country with no specific destination, no deadlines. That was not to be.

In 1997, after several months of acute indigestion, Leroy was diagnosed with esophageal cancer. Six months later my beloved was dead. Those six months tell a love story of their own, but that's for another time.

After Leroy's death I decided to continue my traveling in the RV, and I attended some of our traveling club's events alone. I attended the one in April at the full moon. There were storms throughout that night, high winds, lots of lightning, and heavy rains, and of course, my dear Leroy was strongly on my mind.

Lying there in bed, I became aware of the familiar sound of breathing beside me.

I turned toward that sound, and there next to me was Leroy's beloved face upon his pillow! His radiant face shone brightly in the moonlight. He appeared not as a photograph, but rather as fully three-dimensional. His eyes were gently closed as if he were sleeping peacefully.

I was not afraid or startled by Leroy's presence; I was instantly warmed and strengthened by it. Reaching over with my hands, I gently patted and caressed that precious warm cheek and said, "I love you, Leroy."

Looking away, I looked back again to see if this "apparition" would disappear, but it did not. Seconds, minutes, hours, I do not know. There was no sense of time. I slept then, and when I woke later in the night, he was gone. It was then that I finally, really accepted the fact that indeed Leroy was gone for now, but that it is okay. I know that I am going to be all right. Wherever I am and whatever I decide to do, I will be fine. And I know that my beloved Leroy is alive and well, that his life goes on, and that we will be together again.

I do know love! The love that Leroy and I share flows through me always. It transcends life and death; it reaches out, embracing me, across time and space. It knows no limit.

On life's journey, together

Leading the Way

by Marcia Wegman

Our dramatic landing at eleven thousand feet, high in the Andes where Cuzco Valley lies, turned my thoughts to my son, Kyle. How he would have loved this great adventure into the heart of Peru! Fifteen years earlier, when he was just twelve, my son had died in the crash of a small private plane.

Kyle was very much in my mind and heart later as we visited the many magnificent and magical Inca ruins. In my mind's eye I could imagine him racing up and down the thousands of steps and exploring the fascinating labyrinth of intricately fitted stone walls.

The following night, back in Cuzco, we stayed at a charming small hotel in the heart of the city. Lying in my Dutch cupboard bed, built into the wall, I was fully awake but relaxed with eyes closed, relishing the cozy warmth of my llama-skin cover and contemplating the coming day's adventures.

In this relaxed but wakeful state I became gently aware of light laughing voices somewhere behind my head. Suddenly a young boy materialized before me, dove over the bed, and, laughing merrily, somersaulted onto the floor next to me.

As I recovered from the surprise, I felt someone in the bed next to me. Kyle! Now right by my side, my son lay tucked under the covers with me, wearing striped pajamas. He appeared to be a few years younger that he'd been when he died, and his charming, mischievous smile revealed a missing front tooth.

"Kyle!" I exclaimed as we embraced in a very solid, very warm, very real hug. I stroked his silky blond bangs. "Are you here in Peru with us?"

"Yes," he exclaimed, "I always get to be out in front!" With glorious laughter he disappeared.

Kyle's touch, the feel of his silky blond hair, the sound of his joyful laughter, and the warmth of our loving embrace are still with me. Our precious unexpected reunion reminds me once again what a teacher Kyle has been for me. Because of the depth of my anguish and grief when he died fifteen years ago, I started out on my own spiritual journey. I find that Kyle is always there, out in front, holding my hand and leading the way.

A tender kiss, filled with love, brings comfort and healing

An Indian Morning
by Manoj Soral

On a typically cool December morning in India, I was finding it difficult to wake up, having reached home late the previous night. Grandfather was sitting in the room where I was sleeping. With half-opened eyes, I looked at him, turned over, and went back to sleep, my back now toward my grandfather.

Just then, I felt an unearthly presence bending over me. I knew that it was a woman and wanted to open my eyes, but my body was too relaxed and I couldn't. As the woman moved closer to me, I felt a little afraid for an instant but was unable to do anything about it.

The woman bent still closer and kissed me sweetly on my cheek. Her radiant touch exuded the very essence of love and warmth and caring. The moment she was gone I missed her loving presence.

Able now to sit up, I could see that my grandfather sat gazing at the front door, which faces my room, and together we watched as my mother entered from the other side of the room.

Grandfather said to her, "Your mother has just come by here," speaking of her mother, my grandmother. "She was here. When I saw her walk out the door, at first I thought it was you going out, but then I saw that you were in the kitchen. I looked at her again and realized that it was your mother."

I listened to him and then slowly told them what had happened moments earlier. As I told them how Grandmother had kissed me so lovingly and with such tenderness, all of us became misty eyed, because my dear grandmother had died in 1975.

Soon after this visitation experience, my grandfather himself died at the age of eighty. We felt that Grandmother had come to bid us good-bye before taking Grandfather away with her. Her reassuring touch has been greatly healing for me when I mourn those I love who have passed on.

Her sweet kiss upon my cheek remains one of the most pro-foundly moving experiences of my life.

Unable to resist, she reaches out to embrace her dear friend

The Song of Love

by Sarah Markwell

Before he died, my beloved friend Liam, our choir director and organist, expressed his desire that the members of our choir sing for his funeral mass. Too grief-stricken to sing much at the service, I did very much sense Liam's presence just near the organ throughout the mass.

That night Liam appeared to me in an extraordinary visitation dream, which I can remember vividly to this day.

I was in the parish church along with the other choir members when someone suddenly exclaimed, "Look! There's Liam!"

Turning around, I saw my dear friend standing there before me. Joy filled my heart to see him again, and as I ran to hug him, Liam very lovingly but very emphatically said to me, "Don't touch me!"

Overcome with joy at his presence, I ignored his words and threw my arms around him. I vividly felt the warmth and depth of Liam's love as he disappeared and the dream suddenly ended.

"Don't touch me!" Jesus said the same words at the resurrection. I have many times thought about these words and wondered at their meaning. Does the injunction come for the sake of the embodied person or the person now in spirit? I have no answers.

Liam's visit was quite real and exceedingly comforting to me. While I continue to miss him and grieve for my loss, the comfort of knowing he is safe in spirit brings me much consolation.

A young man returns, able to touch and affect the
material world around him

Riding with Joy

by Frances Sandlin

Our son Brian was killed violently twenty-two years ago.

Brian had bought an old antique car that he planned to restore. He was very mechanically inclined and loved nothing better than to be fixing and driving his cars. So, after our son's death, my husband, Elija, began restoring Brian's favorite old car as a way of feeling closer to his son. Afterward we began using it as a second car.

One day a couple of years after Brian's death, I was out for a walk when his antique car pulled up beside me. I was absolutely stunned to see my dead son, Brian, sitting so naturally behind the steering wheel. It couldn't be! But he was certainly there. Brian signaled for me to get in the car, and when I did he put it into gear and began driving. My son was dead, but here he looked and seemed to be in perfect health and was very much alive.

Brian drove down the road with me sitting right there beside him. We went into the nearby state park and drove around for a while before he took me back to our home. We sat there silently for a few minutes. When I had the thought of reaching over to touch him, Brian implored me, saying, "Please, don't touch me!"

But I was unable to resist, and when I reached out and touched him, Brian was instantly gone. I was left sitting there alone in the passenger seat of the car. Though sorry that I had touched him and caused him to vanish, still, I was more thrilled than I had ever been in my life. It was real—my dear son had been there driving his own car with me sitting right beside him.

Was I dreaming? No, it was not a dream. That ride was real at the time, and today, twenty years later, it is still just as real to me as the day it happened. It was my son. I know with absolute certainty that he's still alive. Brian loved cars so much, and he was always working on them, so it is natural that he would come back to us in his favorite car.

Brian wanted me to know that he is still alive. Because he died violently, he wanted to show me also that his body is undamaged now. He is in perfect health and is still able to do the things he always liked to do.

It's been over twenty years now since that day. My life has changed. Yes, I still grieve for him, but it's different now knowing that we will meet again and that I, too, will live on after my body dies. Every day I thank the Lord for those precious minutes. I remember it today just exactly as if it happened only a few moments ago, and I know that I always will. It is and always will be the most important event of my entire life.

Chapter 8

The Life We Live:
Concerns for Our Daily Lives

Birth, marriage, love, art, religion, war, health, pregnancy, home, career, death, car keys, the senior prom, dinner on Saturday, the new puppy, finding your shoes, rush hour traffic, calling a baby-sitter, minestrone soup—from the archetypal rites of passage to the mundane activities of daily living, our lives are made up of details. Woven together, they form the fabric of our days. From this fabric we fashion a life and from this life we create a destiny.

Navigating the experiences and concerns of life, large and small, for most of us starts early in childhood. Each stage of life, carrying its own timely imperatives, requires that we attend to the never-ending demands of the outer life as well as to the perhaps even more demanding world of our emotional, mental, creative, and spiritual needs. Heart and soul are formed in the brightly burning fire of experience.

It is easy to feel overwhelmed by all the choices we continue to face—choices that will deeply affect us and those we love. We all have longed at times for the guidance of a higher perspective, for the insight to lift our limited vision so it encompasses a broader view of the possibilities and consequences of our choices, for a sense of the larger pattern of our lives.

In many visitations the loved one expresses continuing concern for what we are going through, from the trivial things to the most important, life-changing events. Loved ones in the hereafter seem to know all about our daily lives and express the desire to lovingly guide and help us along our way.

Several years ago I had a visitation from my father in which he expressed concern for my financial problems at the time. After he gave me some valuable parental guidance I expressed my surprise and said, "I didn't know that you would continue, in the afterlife, to have fatherly concern for me. I know that, as a soul, you continue to love me, but I am surprised that you still relate to me as my parent and care about the events of my ordinary, daily life."

"Yes," my father said simply, "some things such as these continue even up to the twelfth level."

At the time his answer made perfect inward sense to me, and though its meaning is still with me, I have never been able to adequately translate that understanding into words. Nonetheless, at that time I became fascinated that our loved ones in the afterlife do indeed seem to know all about our lives and apparently still care about the particular events and occurrences that we encounter.

In the following stories loved ones reach out from the other side to help with many things: they may assist with career choices and changes or encourage an avocation. Sometimes they help us in serving others. They may actively support the growth of character and inner strength. Our departed loved ones often take part in our weddings, pregnancies, illnesses, and family life or bring new pets or remind us to change the oil in the car or show up to give a special recipe. They offer guidance, validation, and reassurance, encouraging us, supporting us, warning and protecting us.

These diverse stories share a common message of comfort for all, whether or not you have ever had a visitation yourself. They reveal that loved ones who have passed over know of our lives, our hopes, and our dreams, and they guide and care for us from the afterlife. Assured that we are never really alone in the large or small things of life, we are encouraged to embrace the fullness of our potential and the possibilities for rich and meaningful life here and now.

Otherworldly support comes to an artist, giving her the courage needed to live a life true to her inner calling

A Life of My Own
by Marion Alfred

When I think back on that first meeting, I feel so grateful. It dramatically altered the course of my life.

I come from a wealthy old eastern family that had the usual expectations, especially in the nineteen forties and fifties when I was growing up. I was expected to follow right into marriage, motherhood, and the Junior League. The only problem was that I wanted to be an artist, a real artist, not one of the acceptable genteel hobbyists taking watercolor classes at the academy.

Trying to make my wishes known to my parents was futile; they were deaf to the idea and assumed it was only a phase. They genuinely could not imagine that anyone, especially a woman, would aspire to anything other than a continuation of their own privileged way of life.

I found it impossible to express my feelings or the real depth of my need to be an artist. After months of trying, I finally gave in and let them convince me to start college first and take some art courses later, along with my other classes. They thought it would give me time to outgrow the whole artist business; I thought it would buy me some time while I figured out how to get their blessing and approval for becoming an artist.

Four years later, without having taken even a single art course, I graduated with honors. I now had both a degree in English literature and a fiancé. I told myself over and over that I was still just buying time until I could get them all to understand me.

In the first year of my marriage I came to the awful realization that, although my desire to be an artist was deeper than ever, I was a coward, unable to assert myself to my parents and now my husband. I became severely depressed and filled with self-contempt. My darkness and depression deepened day by day as I felt my life to be an endless, meaningless trap. At twenty-three, I saw my life as over, and I could see only one way out.

With great calm and resolve I planned to take my own life. I actually felt cheered by the knowledge that I would soon escape my suffocating box. To everyone around me I appeared to be more cheerful, "as a young bride should be," when in fact I was thinking only about how I would end my life.

During this period, I awoke one night just before dawn and heard a woman's voice whisper, "Come with me." Compelled to follow her, I immediately felt the love and strong connection between us. As I went with her into the library, she closed the door behind me.

Once inside, I had the most extraordinary experience of my life. Standing before me was my great-aunt, who had been a renowned artist when she was alive, an impressionist painter. With my unending passion for her work throughout my childhood, I felt that it was she who had inspired me to be a painter.

I cannot say in words exactly how it happened, but there in the library Aunt Marie inflamed my passion for art. More important, she awakened in me the courage and fierce resolve that I had never before had but that she assured me would be an essential ingredient if I were to find a life separate from the expectations and approval of my family. She gave me the vision of what my life could be as an artist. But, she insisted, I had to choose it now and continue to choose it every day of my life. Every action and decision each day, she told me, had to be aligned with my purpose and direction.

My choice was made before I left the library that night. Three months later I left my husband and family and moved to Paris. With no one's approval and very little money, I began my serious study of art. That was over forty years ago.

I have no regrets.

Urging a young man to release his doubts and embrace wholeheartedly the new direction of his life and work

On the Path

by Paul Butterfield

When I decided to leave the family business and go to acupuncture school, my parents and family thought I was crazy. Though feeling in my heart that it was what I really wanted to do, because of my family's angry and negative reaction, some part of me still wondered if I was making a big mistake.

Rejected by my family, I suffered in the following weeks and months from overwhelming inner conflict and uncertainty. One night, in the midst of my confusion, I had a dream.

In the fading light I stood on a small bridge looking out over a large, fog-covered pond. I sensed a powerful spirit in the distance, coming toward me from across the water. He came to me quickly in three movements and appeared in front of me.

I started crying with wonder and amazement when I knew that it was my oldest and dearest friend, my beloved grandfather. Grandfather looked at me with infinite love and compassion and said simply, "You're on the right path, you are doing the right thing, keep going."

Without speaking aloud, I pleaded with him to stay, to tell me more, all the while somehow knowing that he could not remain or say more. I knew he would soon be gone.

"You're on the right path, you are doing the right thing, keep going." Again he spoke, with the greatest love and kindness I had ever known.

He silently acknowledged my tears, my wanting him to stay, my desire to be with him. Though he had to go, Grandfather let me know that everything was unfolding according to a larger plan.

A third and final time, Grandfather repeated his words: "You're on the right path, you are doing the right thing, keep going." Then, with three quick movements back across the misty pond, he was gone.

I awakened, crying with my whole being. Beside me, my lover awoke, asking what was the matter. Through my tears I replied that I had just been with my best friend throughout all eternity, my grandfather, who had died when I was seven.

After my dream I was able to effortlessly let go of all doubt about the life choice I made. My grandfather's loving spirit came to me when I needed him and let me know that he supported the important and difficult decision that I was making about my life's work.

It is never too late to see new possibilities that can lead to greater fulfillment

The Village Doctor
by Christian Messerli

My father, when he was alive, always wanted me to continue his general medical practice in the village near Berne, Switzerland, where he lived, but I was too young then and had not finished my postgraduate education. I went on to become a pulmonary specialist. I was never totally happy with my choice, as this specialty has been somewhat difficult for me. I am now over sixty years old and have felt for a long time that it is too late to make a significant change, and so I have been resigned to my unhappy situation. Until now. My father came to me in a dream just two days ago.

In the dream I felt myself to be enchanted. I was with him in his own house. "Father," I said to him, "I think it's soon time for you to finish working as a doctor. You are already rather old."

My father replied, "I have thought already a long time of finishing, and I wait now only for you to take over my practice."

His reply surprised me. I was at the same time glad and embarrassed to hear his words. I answered him, "This is a good occasion for ending my practice and beginning a new one because it is no longer going well in the town. But, Father, it would take a great deal to do to make such a change." I went on, seeing only the obstacles, "I am not so sure that everything would go well. Are there not already enough doctors in the village? Surely it might be difficult to start again, to establish my new practice. I don't know if I could accustom myself to those new circumstances now at my sixty-one years."

"Change the style of your practice," my father counseled me. "Be more a general practitioner, not only a specialist. Do not worry, you will see that your practice will flower." He assured me that it would go well for me.

My father had come back after all these years to counsel me one more time to take over his practice. He seemed to know that I had not been comfortable in my current situation but had been feeling that it was too late to make a change. My father is telling me that it is not too late, trying to encourage me to go in a new direction that will bring me greater happiness.

I was left with a good, hopeful feeling from his visit; I felt my father's encouragement. It was such a timely and meaningful dream, and when I woke up, I felt like I was enchanted.

With advice, guidance, and support, he is blessed each day while going about his work

A Light unto My Spirit
by the Reverend Marion Blair

My foster mother is my frequent visitor and has been for all of the years since her death. She usually appears early in the morning, awakening me and giving me a message of peace, wellness, joy, sorrow, caution, or danger. Often these messages are given to me to share with other people or to guide me through times of trouble, fear, or uncertainty.

Her messages are clear, direct, and prescriptive. She has been a light unto my spirit and a guide unto my feet. Because of this light, twenty-one years ago, I accepted a call as minister, pastor, and teacher. During my tenure as a college student, military officer, probation officer, husband, father, teacher, businessman, and pastor, the impact of my mother's guidance from the other world has changed and continues to change my life and the lives of people I seek to serve. Her light is a frequent and welcome visitor to me.

My first visitation experience was many years ago when I was a young child growing up in a foster home. My foster mother, the Reverend Mary L. Blair (the first African American woman ordained to preach in an A.M.E. Zion church), was the assistant pastor of St. Mark's Church.

The evening was quiet, and our church was to celebrate the Holy Communion. Suddenly, from the candle-lighted chancel and pews, a brilliant light appeared! This light hovered over and around my mother. She suffered from advanced arthritis and moved very slowly. When this light bathed her body, she seemed to take wings. She moved down the right aisle of the building, across the back, and up the left aisle, and her feet did not touch the floor, as if she were being carried by a mighty wind. I had never seen such a brilliant light, too bright to look into and emitting a warmth that filled the church.

Years later, when my mother died, this joyous and beautiful light returned to me, appearing as her beloved face.

My mom visits with me as I minister in the homes, churches, schools, and hospitals. She is keenly aware of the circumstances and events of my life and of the lives of those to whom I minister, and she is able to pass along her guidance and advice and blessing when we are in need.

To live my dreams while living in the world

Learning to Fly

by Lee Lawson

Grandfather Moore died two months before I was born. I've often wondered if the existential questions that were in my heart even as I was being born, even before words, might have come, in part, from this epic passage in my mother's life. Her beloved father was dying and leaving this world while she herself was pregnant and ready to birth a child into the world. These mythic events being held in the same heart at the same moment surely helped to turn my view toward the matters of life and death and the soul.

As a child of five, I sat on the back porch furiously coloring away with my crayons when I noticed him the first time. He just stood in the doorway, gazing at me lovingly from across the room. He smiled; I smiled and went back to my important work.

I knew at the time that this silent man in the doorway was not "there" like other people were there. I don't know how I knew but I did, and I also knew, instinctively, that this was not something to be spoken of to anyone else. It felt special, to be shared with no one, especially not my family members, all of whom were preoccupied with the daily demands of family life in the 1950s.

Over the next five years, I came to know the quiet man in the doorway as we communicated—silently at first, in silent words and many silent pictures. I never knew when to expect him; he would just be there, not all the time, only sometimes. Always I was alone, often making a picture with colors from the crayon box or a little later painting or walking in the woods. Slowly and very gently, we began to get to know each other.

Being with him was comforting and easy, and I looked forward to being together because we entered a wonderful world composed of ideas and colors, philosophy and dreams. In that world, I was not five or six or seven years old. I was not a child or adult.

Over the years of Grandfather's visits, I was learning from him a kind of spiritual and emotional self-reliance. It enabled me to grow as an artist within a family and a culture focused entirely on the outer world, among people who had little connection with the existence or needs of the soul.

When he was alive, Grandfather had been a dreamer, a pilot, engineer, and inventor. His first love was flying, and he worked his way through college as a barnstormer, flying around to many communities outside of Chicago in his small airplane, taking people up for rides.

His life as dreamer and adventurer essentially ended when he married my grandmother, who was a student at the Art Institute of Chicago.

With marriage, both put dreams aside and entered into what was for each of them the too-small confines of family life. Not surprisingly, as Grandfather put away his dreams, he eventually became an alcoholic.

Grandfather's intermittent visits over a period of about five years gave me a sense of being deeply connected with the unseen. Even as a young child, I had a strong sense of the inner life, and he confirmed for me that there was a much greater world than the one I could see. My own life was grounded in that knowledge, and it became the foundation of all that has come since. Grandfather served as an anchor, teaching me to live in the material world with all of its requirements without being swept up by the endless demands of the culture as he had been. He wanted me to be able to complete that which he and generations before him had been unable to do—to be strong enough to hold my own vision of my life and destiny and to fulfill my dreams to be an artist. Imparting to me a kind of ferocity, he gave me a way to safeguard and protect the things that are important to me, without being bitter or estranged from the world around me.

Grandfather Moore's last visitation came when I was almost ten. I didn't know at the time that I wouldn't see him again. I knew that he was pleased with my resolve to live a life according to the dictates of my spirit, even at that early age, and he felt assured that I had the inner strength and passion to persevere.

Grandfather brought me that far, and then I had to fly on my own.

Joyful that her family will be whole and loved, she gives her blessing

Family Blessing
by Julia Schmucker

Don and I began dating six years after the death of his wife, Linda. Now I was faced with the decision of whether or not to marry. I felt that our marriage was in the stars, but many questions caused me uncertainty. Don had children (and an ex-wife) from a first marriage as well as a daughter, Kathryn, from his marriage to Linda. Would the children accept me? Could I ever feel comfortable in Linda's home using her things, being mother to her daughter? Could I ever find my true place among so many seemingly conflicting imperatives? All these concerns and more swirled in my heart as I tried to decide what to do. I loved Don and wanted to be with him, but the rest was all so confusing.

Everyone else was asleep one night when I was inwardly summoned into the second bedroom. There I soon found myself sitting across from Linda! As I sat on the bed, wide awake, Linda (whom I had never met when she was alive) sat in the rocking chair near me.

Although I couldn't say if we sat there for two hours or only a moment, she and I had a conversation that changed my life. She lovingly asked me to take care of Donald and their child, Kathryn. She wanted me to adopt her daughter, but only when Kathryn was ready. Linda gave me her blessing to marry Donald and become a real mother to Kathryn.

Not just giving me her blessing, she expressed deep gratitude and relief that I wanted to become a part of her family and love and care for the people she loved the most. It felt as though a terrible weight had been lifted from my shoulders.

She told me not to be anxious about Donald's first wife, that it would not be a problem for us. Linda seemed to know all that was on my mind and causing me so much worry and confusion.

I have never felt Linda's presence again, but my husband has and it is comforting to him and never intrusive. Linda has given us a wonderful gift in giving her blessing to our family and in watching over us to this day.

With us through all of the important times and events of our lives

My Wedding Day
by Gloria Owens

The month leading up to my wedding was an unusually stressful time. After planning and unplanning and planning again, I had so much to think about and so much to do.

Could I let go of trying to control everything about the day enough to relax and enjoy my own wedding? Control was the issue, my lifelong issue.

Control I learned from my father. From him I learned how to get things done—the way they should be done, of course. In retrospect I can see that I spent a lot of energy trying to get good grades or win a medal to gain his approval and his apparently very conditional love. There was a part of me that never fully felt loved by him.

I did not understand this unfinished business between Dad and me when he died suddenly of a heart attack during my senior year of college. As I mourned his death over the next few years, he would occasionally show up in my dreams, usually just to say, "Hey, everything's okay, you're on the right track," or "Don't forget to change the oil in your car!" He always seemed to know when I was neglecting my car.

Over the years his memory became more distant, and I focused on other things. It was through my practice of yoga that I learned to cultivate awareness and acceptance, yet I was always struggling with the duality of control and surrender. Surrender meant trust and willingness to accept every moment as it is. My father's voice, the voice of control, became a limiting tape in my head, as I struggled to be more intuitive, more trusting, and more open in my life.

The morning of our wedding day I had hoped to sleep in since the ceremony was not until early evening. Instead, I found myself awakening to the sounds of birds outside my window at 6 A.M. At first I thought I was still asleep, for I felt myself surrounded by a soft pink light that illuminated everything in the room. I didn't feel the weight of my body on the bed. Instead, I felt like I was being carried in a soft, warm pink blanket.

All at once my father was there with me, holding me in a fully loving embrace. I did not have to see his physical form to know from the depths of my soul that he was carrying me. I was being supported and rocked by him as I awoke into the day.

Tears of joy overwhelmed me and soaked my pillow. I relaxed into my father's total embrace. Pure, unconditional love permeated every cell of my body, with energy, trust, knowing, and joy!

My father came to bless me, to bless my marriage, and to bless my life with unconditional love. He wanted me to know that I could let go, I didn't have to prove anything, I didn't have to earn love. The tug-of-war had ended. I could simply be myself. It was enough.

My father's precious wedding gift to me that day changed my life forever, because it changed the way I live each day.

I no longer have to earn love. There are still days when I walk the line between control and surrender, between doing and not doing, but I no longer have to control the events and people in my life and I am more able to let life unfold in all of its beauty and grace.

Knowing now that her father is always there with her, right by her side

Birth into Life

by Karen Dougherty

I cried often. Twenty-three years old and eight months pregnant when my father died, I was very distraught and felt that he'd left me alone when I still needed him so badly in my life.

One night just before sleep I heard a phone ringing, but it wasn't my phone. The ringing was within me, yet it was so clear that I sat up in bed and said out loud, "Hello?"

With that my father suddenly appeared, almost fully formed yet transparent, at the foot of my bed! He had no feet but rather faded out below the knees. I was so thrilled and happy to see him.

He spoke to me telepathically, saying that he loved me dearly. He told me not to cry anymore, that he was with me still, and that he would always be there for me. Happier now than he ever had been when he was alive, he didn't want me to grieve for him anymore.

I told my father how much I loved him, and as quickly as that it was over. Things were just as they had been. My father was dead. But in our precious minutes together he let me know that I will not go through my days without him. He is with me here and now and will forever be a part of my life. I felt such joy as I had never known.

Two weeks after that, after a very easy labor, my baby girl came into the world. Throughout the delivery I felt his presence, and at the very moment of birth the ceiling above me opened up before my eyes, and there was my glowing father smiling lovingly down at me. My daughter was born on February 2, my father's birthday!

Our daily happiness is important to our loved ones in spirit

Pascadeli Soup
by Marissa Cavanaugh

My grandmother, who'd recently died, walked down the hallway and into my bedroom, where we had a wonderful and joyous reunion. I thought that I was sitting up in bed, though in reality I was still asleep and having the most extraordinary dream of my entire life.

"Nonnie," I asked her, "why are you dressed like that?"

"What do you mean, Marissa?" she asked.

I said, "Well, I know that you're in heaven. I thought you were suppose to wear a long, white dress or something like that. Something heavenly."

With a loving smile Nonnie told me, "You can wear whatever you want here." Looking exactly as I remembered her, except a bit more beautiful, she was dressed just as she always was when she was alive: nylon pants, always a bit short, and her nylon top.

Grandmother reached out her hand to me, and I put my hand in hers without question or apprehension. We talked for a time about some particular family matters, and she assured me, "Yes, I know all about what is going on in the family, Marissa. Don't be concerned. Things will work out in their own time. You must be patient."

Then she wanted to tell me something quickly. She said, "Marissa, I know Amanda loves the soup that I make. I want to give you my special recipe." I instantly knew what she was talking about. Grandmother cooked for my daughter in the past, and

Amanda did indeed love her pascadeli soup. It's a soup she made for years with bread crumbs and eggs and smelly Italian cheese.

Prior to that night, I had a general idea of how to make the soup, but here she was, giving me her complete recipe. She told me several of her key, secret ingredients; I had not known that the soup needed juice and rind of lemon, also nutmeg.

After she gave me her recipe, I hugged my grandmother and asked her if she could come and visit me like this from time to time, "to check up, you know, chat and catch up on family things."

Saying that she didn't believe she could come back, Nonnie told me, "It gets harder to come back." Wiping a tear away from my eye, she smiled the most beautiful smile I have ever seen, and then she was gone.

I awoke from my grandmother's visitation with full memory of her recipe. It was an incredible experience and fills me with joy to know that my grandmother continues not only to love us, but also to be concerned about our health and happiness in our day-to-day lives.

Pascadeli soup will never be the same.

Loving intercession from the afterlife

Just the Right One
by Janet Ziegler

When our family dog died, my children desperately wanted another one. Two of my sons were in high school and the other in college, so I didn't want to take on the responsibility of another animal. They tried to get a dog "for their dad" a number of times, but I vetoed it every time.

One day when my son was home from college, the three boys headed out for the library, leaving me alone in the house. I was delighted to have some peace and quiet for a while and decided I would take the time to meditate.

As I sat quietly I heard a voice. "It's time you let those children have another dog." It was the voice of my sister, Alice, who'd died a few years before.

"Alice, I do not want another animal," I told her emphatically. "I want some freedom to travel when the boys leave for college." On I went, giving her all my reasons for saying no.

Insisting just as emphatically that this was a perfect time for us to get a new dog, my sister insisted that the family, especially the boys, really needed one.

"Easy for you to say," I replied, "you're dead. You don't have to take care of it!"

"Well, I'm going to send you just the right one, anyway." And with that, Alice disappeared.

Minutes later, I heard the boys return. In ahead of them ran a little bundle of fur. A golden retriever puppy jumped up into my lap and looked right at me, her eyes saying loud and clear, "I'm the one!"

What could I do? I rarely argued with my sister in life, so how could I argue with her in death? The boys kept the dog, and I made sure they knew it was only through the intercession of their aunt that their wish came true! As it turned out, the puppy—we named her Sheana—was indeed "just the right one." She seemed to know all the house rules and has blessed us with many years of joy and happiness.

Chapter 9

Guardians:
Protection, Guidance, and Warning

Wake up! Turn around! Stop the car! Call home! The warnings given by caring visitors from the afterlife can sometimes save people from death, danger, or calamity. Warning, protection, and rescue are the central themes of the selections in this chapter. These visitations are for the sole purpose of keeping someone safe and out of harm's way. The stories tell us again and again that not only are the details of our daily lives known on the other side, but also that it is sometimes possible to reach across the dimensions and make a difference in the flow of events.

I have chosen a variety of stories to show the many ways in which loved ones from the afterlife can protect us. From preventing a sexual assault to rescuing a child from drowning, each story portrays a timely intervention that prevents serious injury or death. Each visitation, expressed in a very personal and meaningful way, was compelling enough to prevent injury or harm coming to someone involved in a potentially dangerous situation.

You might think that anyone would take heed if someone from the hereafter issued an urgent warning, but I am amazed at how often people ignore such a warning until it has been said several times at an ever-escalating volume. Personally, I would need to hear it only once if my father suggested that I get out of the rocking chair—now!

The timing in each of these stories is interesting. In the first four stories the visitation comes just before the threatening event, by just seconds or a few minutes. In the fifth story, of the near-drowning, the intervention comes during the event, and in the final story, the warning arrives a few days before the crisis point of the experience.

After hearing many stories, I am inclined to believe that while those in the afterlife cannot necessarily prevent certain things from happening—a tree falling, an illness, a robbery—what they can sometimes do is adjust or change your part in the event. The land-slide may still happen, but you won't be under it.

We cannot help but wonder why help comes to one person and not another, why now, why here. This is one of the unfathomable mysteries that, I believe, is outside of our present understanding. What we do know for certain is that sometimes someone slips through the veil just in time to be of help and in the process leaves us, one and all, in a wistful state of awe and wonder.

Unlikely protectors bring a life lesson in a hurry

One Saturday Night

by Catherine Jones

When I was a girl of fifteen, I went along with my friend one Saturday night on a baby-sitting job in her apartment complex. As we were sitting quite late, I made plans to stay over at my friend's house for the night.

That evening there came a knock at the door and a man's voice saying that he was a friend of the woman for whom we were sitting. My friend did not want to answer the door, but after much insis-tence from me—after all, the man said that he had traveled far on his motorcycle and was tired—she reluctantly agreed to open it.

Though my friend was quite unnerved and skeptical about him, the man came inside. I, on the other hand, was impressed and excited with his stories and flattered by the attention that he paid to me. He was much older than we were.

After a short visit the stranger invited me to go for a ride on his motorcycle. I was thrilled by his invitation. I had never even sat on a motorcycle before, and now this much older, interesting man was paying a lot of attention to me and offering to give me a ride on his!

Completely ignoring my friend's objections, I went along with him. We climbed onto the motorcycle and drove off. We didn't get very far, though, just behind the building in the nearby woods. There the man pulled over and immediately began to remove my clothes and fondle me.

Shocked and terrified, I began praying for help. I was crying as I prayed. Then, very suddenly, everything stopped.

The man looked at me as if he were seeing a ghost and then stopped attacking me. Telling me to get back on the motorcycle, he said that he would take me back to the apartment.

Badly shaken, I went back inside. With absolutely no idea why the attack had ended so suddenly, I was just grateful to be safely inside once again.

The next day while lying in my bed at home—I was wide awake—my aunt Marge appeared out of nowhere, standing at the foot of the bed. My aunt had passed on many years before. Behind her and to my left stood another woman whom I did not recognize.

Aunt Marge did all the talking. Pointing her finger as if to scold me, she said that it was really a shame that you can't trust people like I wanted to, but that I had to learn to be more cautious in my life or I was likely to get into some real trouble next time.

Then they were gone.

Racing downstairs, I told my mother, "I just saw Aunt Marge and some other lady!" And I described the other woman.

Just as calmly as could be, my mother said, "Oh, that other lady was my mother."

I had never met my maternal grandmother or even seen a picture of her. She had died when my mother was only twelve years old.

Now, some thirty years later, I am still accused of seeing the world through rose-colored glasses. I haven't lost that quality of trust that I possess, though it is now blended with the use of caution, as Aunt Marge and my grandmother so strongly and lovingly suggested.

Together through the storm

Best Friends
by Paula M. Oberne

A fierce coastal storm came up in the middle of the night, and the wind was howling loudly enough to wake me up. My two dogs were still sleeping next to me, oblivious to the increasing storm outside. I lay awake. The sounds of the wind and the rain made a strange and beautiful music, and I listened, enchanted by its eerie beauty. I knew that no hurricanes were predicted, so, feeling very warm and safe in my own bed, I was enjoying every minute of relaxation.

At first I thought it was just the trees creaking in the wind, but as it continued I gradually became aware that someone was speaking to me. "It's me, it's Wendy." She giggled with the conspiratorial laughter that I loved so when she was alive. We melted into each other with the joy and laughter we had when we were two little girls jumping on the bed so many years ago.

After a few minutes Wendy reluctantly became more serious. "I'm here for a reason," she said, "and it's important."

It took me a few seconds to adjust to the serious tone of her voice. She went on, "You need to take the dogs and go into the other room, and you should do it pretty soon." I was amazed that she sounded just like herself, just like before her death.

"Come on." She was suddenly standing in the doorway motioning me to follow. "You should do it right now."

I woke the dogs and headed them both through the door, and we all went downstairs behind Wendy. Not knowing where she wanted us to go, we followed her into my husband's tiny office at the far end of the house. It was starting to dawn on me that I wasn't in my warm bed anymore. It was cold!

I had the thought that I should go back for a blanket and Wendy said, "No, you don't have time, come on."

Once inside the office, she closed the door and we all sat down on the small sofa. I found a coat and wool scarf and put them on. It was dark in the office, but, just as in the bedroom, I could see Wendy as though in candlelight. The minute we settled in, the winds picked up and the howling increased dramatically. I must have fallen asleep right away, because the next thing I knew, I was waking up and it was dawn. Going to the window for my first look at the storm damage, I saw the street was strewn with trees and limbs. People were already out checking on the damage to their cars and houses.

When I opened the office door, a prayer of gratitude flooded through me. A huge pine tree had come down through the roof and landed in the bedroom and the living room. It was an unbelievable mess, and rain was coming in through the roof. At first I thought I was dreaming, because I could not imagine that anyone on earth could have slept through the crash, but I had.

Almost nothing in the bedroom was left in one piece.

My closest friend since grade school, Wendy died at the age of thirty-seven after years of serious kidney disease. We remain the best of friends to this day.

A dramatic intervention protects the people he loves

Going Home

by Melvin Freer

Just last year we were on our way home from shopping one night around seven. My wife, Jean, was driving, and I was telling her about the new law case I had started that day. Instead of going home the usual way, Jean turned onto the freeway. When I asked her why, she glanced at me like I was a little crazy and said, "Because you just asked me to."

"I did no such thing," I protested. "What are you talking about?"

"You said, 'Turn here,' so I did."

We were just about to start debating who was crazy and who wasn't when we both heard a voice—and it did sound like mine—say, "Get off at the Bayshore exit."

At the same time that we heard the voice, the whole inside of the car filled up with a glowing, cloudlike mist that smelled like roses, not overpowering but definitely roses.

Jean exited at Bayshore and continued driving for about five minutes more. Then we heard, "You can go on home now."

She pulled into a parking lot, turned around, and we drove back toward the house. We must have been spellbound, for we just rode along in silence the whole time. About two miles from the house, the voice came again, saying that everything would be all right. This time it was clear that it was my father's voice. Dad died in 1986.

"What in the world—?" I started to say, when suddenly he appeared in the backseat, not fully formed but appearing from the waist up and somewhat transparent.

My dad looked wonderful, robust and alive like I'd never seen him in life, especially in his last years. Looking like a lantern glowing from the inside, he radiated love. That's the only way I can say it. Love radiated from him, and Jean and I were surrounded by it. The love had substance, like oxygen or water. I have never felt such a sense of joy in my life. It was like food to someone starving who didn't even know he was hungry. It was more than my father's love; it was *love*.

He sat there smiling for a minute before he said, "Don't be upset when you get home. There's been a break-in, but they're gone now. Please listen to me carefully. Go in, get your medicine and some clothes, and go right back out and find a motel for tonight. When you are in the room, then phone the police from there." I was looking at him, and I could hear everything he was saying, but for some reason it was hard for me to focus on it.

"Everything will be all right, but hurry."

Jean and I went into the house, which, sure enough, just like he said, had been torn apart. It looked more like vandalism than robbery, but we didn't stop to figure it out. We got a few things together and left.

Dad wasn't in the car when we got in, though there was still the faintest fragrance of roses. I was charged with electricity and I know that my wife was, too, but we were both peaceful nonetheless and just concentrated on following my father's instructions.

We got a motel room and carried our small bag inside. "I'm going outside to lock up the car," I started to tell Jean, when I was interrupted by Dad's voice.

"Okay. Call the police right *now!* Tell them that there is a robbery in progress."

I turned around, went directly to the bedside phone, and dialed the police. As peculiar as this may sound under the circumstances, when I put down the phone, both Jean and I lay down on the bed and fell asleep.

About two hours later we were awakened when the police came to tell us what had happened. When they'd arrived at the house, the perpetrators had already returned and were in the process of loading up some of the things they'd apparently seen on their first entrance. We found out later that they were working for a man whom I had helped send to prison over a year earlier; he had instructed them to trash the house and rough us up a little. A bit of a thank-you note, I imagine.

The perpetrators were also wanted on several other charges, so the police were happy with the evening's work. Jean and I were happy that thanks to my father's intervention we had not been there during either of the visits. We had to do some major cleaning up, but there was not much real damage at the house. I'd been talking about retiring for over five years, so we decided to turn the cleaning to good use and put the house on the market.

Three months later I retired and we moved to our little summer place, where I am growing my roses and Jean is reading all the books she never had time for. Best thing that ever happened to us. We're on a second honeymoon.

Saved from drowning, a boy learns a secret from the past

By Hudson's Creek

by Horace Clifford

Corky and I went down to the creek, even though Mama told me never go there alone. Corky's ball fell in the water, and he was making little sharp barking sounds without it. It was my fault because I threw the ball hard and he couldn't catch it. So we left the backyard just for a minute to get the ball. We would come right back.

A little way into the water was enough to reach the ball, so I got my shoes and socks off and climbed down the bank. Corky stayed there because he never liked going into water. If I slipped or what, I don't know. It happened so fast. I was just under the water, more surprised than anything, not scared even. It felt sort of like I could see myself on television while I was down there.

After a minute I wanted to get out, but I couldn't move. There were branch tangles and roots all over me, and I got really scared then because I couldn't stand up. The water was much deeper than it was when I came down here before, once when Mama let my two cousins bring me here if they promised not to let go of my hand. It only came up to my knees that time. And it wasn't moving very much. It was deep this time, and it was pushing me hard down to the bottom.

The next thing I knew, I was out of the creek, being carried by an old man toward the house. He kept saying, "It's okay, boy," over and over. "It's okay, boy, you're gonna be all right. It's okay, boy."

I could hear myself breathing and my heart pounding in my chest.

We stopped outside the house, and the old man called out, "Betsy! Come out here, Betsy. Your boy needs you."

Mama came running out the door screaming, "Oh, my God! What did you do to him? Put him down! Don't you hurt my son! Horace, are you all right, honey?"

"I pulled your boy out of Hudson's Creek, Betsy." The old man put me down easy onto the ground, turned around, and walked away.

Mama was yelling and crying, "If you've hurt him I'll be calling the sheriff. Leave me and my boy alone, and don't come here again!"

She was hugging me and crying and yelling at him all at the same time. Corky was licking at the water on my feet. Mama took me into the house and changed my clothes and put me in her bed.

From the bed I could hear her talking on the phone, crying and arguing with my grandma. When it got real quiet, I was thinking I wanted to get up and see some television, but Mama had said stay in bed.

Maybe I was sleeping, and when I woke up the sun was almost gone and I was hungry. I went to find Mama. She was sitting on the porch steps with her hands covering her face, crying hard but not making any sounds at all. Her body was shaking all over.

"Mama, I'm okay. Mama. That man didn't hurt me. Mama, Corky's ball went in the creek so we went down there so I could get it out and give it back. I didn't mean to fall in, Mama. It was Corky's ball. Don't cry, Mama. That man. He didn't hurt me. Please don't be mad at me, Mama."

Mama just stared at me like she didn't hear me while I went on and on and on. Finally she pulled me onto her lap and rocked me back and forth while she cried and kissed the top of my hair.

When I asked her who the old man was who carried me to the house, she just started crying again.

We went into the kitchen, and Mama sat down at the table and pulled me up on her lap again.

"The old man, Horace, he was your granddaddy. My daddy."

I didn't even know I had a granddaddy! I had Mama and Daddy and Grandma and Granny Clifford and the people from church. That's all.

"Before you were born, my daddy was unhappy because I wanted to marry your daddy. He didn't like your daddy, so he was real mad and told me not to come back there ever again. So he never got to see you." She started crying again. "My mother, that's your grandma, she came out here to visit without him, so I never saw him for six years now, since your daddy and I married and since you were born." Mama stopped talking for a long time and stared at the floor.

"When I saw my daddy today I was just real surprised and thought he might have hurt you. I understand now that he helped you out of the creek. Horace, I know he didn't hurt you any."

"Mama, Corky's ball fell in the creek and I was just . . . I didn't mean to . . . it was an accident." Now I was crying.

"Horace, it's okay. It's okay, honey, it's okay. I'm not mad at you. Everything is all right." There was the littlest bit of a smile on her face.

I think I fell asleep sitting there on her lap in the kitchen.

She never said another thing about that day or about my grand-daddy ever again.

Six years later, when I was almost twelve, on the night after Mama's funeral, my grandma told me. She said, "That time you fell in the creek and your mama saw her daddy—oh, how that girl loved her daddy when she was a little thing—well, he had died in his sleep the night before. And it was the next day he pulled you out of Hudson's Creek. Horace, when your mama got so sick, that's why she wasn't afraid about dying, and she didn't want you to be afraid either."

Demanding the medical care needed because of an insistent warning

Watching from Afar

by Diane Suissa

My friend Donald came to me from the other side and saved my life.

My husband and I were attending a Greek Orthodox christening on Sunday when I realized I didn't feel well. Later on that night as I slept, I had an extraordinary dream in which my friend Donald came to me, insisting, "Diane! Get up now!" He said that I was going to be very sick and needed to wake up.

Too tired to get up, I moaned, "I just want to sleep," but he interrupted me three times with his demand. Finally, I reluctantly opened my eyes.

It was about four in the morning, and I was so disturbed by my dream and by Donald's vivid presence that I woke my sleeping husband to tell him about it.

The last time I saw Donald was in Chicago, May 1990. I watched him catch a cab, knowing that I was never going to see him again. My dear friend Donald, who had AIDS, died not too long after that day. Seeing him in my dream and feeling the intensity of his concern for me, I was deeply shaken.

My fever was 102.6 degrees when I woke up, not very high but high enough that I didn't feel well. I went back to bed for that whole day, feeling like I just had a mild case of the flu.

In the middle of the next night, I awoke with a fever of almost 104 degrees. Because of the dream and Donald's warning—and only because of it—I asked my husband to take me to the emergency room. But by the time I got to the hospital my fever had dropped below 103.

The emergency room doctor diagnosed a simple case of flu and sent me home.

In the morning, my husband had to leave for work, so I spent the day alone, resting. My concerns should have been allayed by the doctor's words, but they weren't. Still feeling uneasy because of the dream, I didn't really want to be alone. With growing certainty that I needed to heed the dream's message, finally, after many hours, I called my husband and asked him to come home.

When he took my temperature it was almost 105 degrees! He called the doctor's office and I heard the nurse argue with him, saying that I had simply gone from having a mild case of the flu to having a bad case of the flu. She didn't want to disturb the doctor.

Because I could still strongly feel the intensity of Donald's concern, I knew that I needed help, and I insisted that we go to the emergency room—again—regardless of what the nurse said. When we arrived, my temperature had climbed up past 106, and they discovered I had pneumonia.

Under ordinary circumstances, I never would have been alerted to the fact that I had anything other than the flu, and I'm certain I never would have gone to a hospital emergency room twice with the flu, no matter how sick I felt. Donald's concern caused me to pay attention and demand the care that I needed. Indeed, his warning from the other side saved my life.

Watching over her beloved school

Miss Hadley's Children
by Charlotte R. Turner

My first teaching job was at Hadley Elementary School in a tiny three-room rural schoolhouse. The students were divided into two groups: my group of first, second, and third graders and Lydia's fourth, fifth, and sixth graders. The schoolhouse was originally an old church building converted into classrooms by the town's first official teacher in 1926, over thirty years earlier, to serve the small village and surrounding farming community.

We were feeling the chill of mid-October, poised on the brink of winter. Only the week before, a new, modern gas furnace had been installed at the schoolhouse, finally replacing the decrepit one, which had needed replacing for at least ten years. That ancient boiler furnace hadn't been dependable for heat for a while, and it made terrible noises that frightened children and teachers alike. After endless pestering by worried parents, the district council finally had a new, modern gas furnace installed.

Tuesday after lunch, when we were having our weekly art session, a woman burst into the classroom and, addressing the children directly, said, "Now, children, go as quickly and quietly as you can, take your coats, and go outside to the benches on the far side of the field and stay there until I tell you to come back. Now go, quickly. Right now!" The children stood up immediately and started for their coats.

The woman was calm, but the urgency in her voice was clear. She spoke with absolute authority, so much so that I found myself saying, "Now hurry up, children, let's go outside, quickly," as I started herding the class out the door. I didn't stop to wonder who she was.

As we got the last child through the door and into the field, the woman turned to me. "Make sure that all your children are there with you, and stay there. I am going for Lydia's group. Now hurry!" I marched my baffled children across the field in the cold, crisp chill air. As we went, I could hear Lydia and the woman talking excitedly and then sounds of the older children leaving the classroom to follow us.

Her voice more urgent now, the woman hurried the older children through the door, ordering them to go quickly to the benches. "Now, take Flora's hand and run over to the bench," she called out to one child as she herself grabbed the hand of one of the other smaller girls. Lydia was half running, half walking alongside the children, saying, "You don't understand . . . impossible . . . it's less than a week old!"

In less than a minute we were all gathered at the benches about fifty yards from the schoolhouse. Lydia and the woman were speaking, both animated and insistent. "But you don't understand, Augusta. The furnace was replaced. There's a new one now. It's perfectly safe. It's brand new."

"Lydia! You aren't listening to me! The furnace is going to explode! *Do not* take these children back into that school!"

Oh, now I understand, I remember thinking, she must be one of the grandparents who was worried about the furnace and doesn't know that they put in a new one last week.

With a look of exasperation on her face, Lydia was trying to convince the woman that the old, dangerous furnace was gone. Trying to stay calm, Lydia went on, "I know that your concern is for the children, Augusta, but there is nothing to worry about. It's cold out here, and I need to get these children back inside. Some of them are out here without coats. This school is my responsi—"

"Listen to me! I will not have any of my children hurt, do you understand me? I will not!" At that very instant, the schoolhouse exploded and burst into flames.

Thirty-four gaping students and two astonished teachers were riveted to the spot, watching in horror as the school burned before our eyes. Lydia sent two of the older boys to get help.

We were counting the students when help came and along with it most of the people from the town and surrounding area. It didn't take long for them to discover that the furnace had been installed improperly and had a faulty gas valve on the pipe that led from the tank. The new furnace blew up the school! The irony was lost on no one.

After a confusing, exhausting day, I finally got home in the early evening, ready to sleep for a week. At only seven o'clock, I was already in bed with a cup of tea when the doorbell rang. My husband answered it, brought Lydia back into the bedroom, and pulled up the rocking chair next to the bed so she could sit down beside me.

When Tom left the room, Lydia and I just looked at each other and started to cry. Our tears were a mixture of exhaustion and relief . . . what if . . . thank God . . .

"Thank God for that grandmother" were my first words. "She saved our lives."

"That's why I'm here, Charlotte." Lydia was choked up, and it was difficult for her to speak. "That wasn't one of the grandparents. That was Augusta Hadley. She was the teacher who started the school back in the twenties."

"But I thought Mrs. Hadley was dead," I interrupted.

Looking down for a minute, Lydia started to cry again. "She is."

When she was calmer, Lydia told me that the night before, she'd dreamed of Augusta Hadley warning her that the school was in danger, that the furnace was going to blow up. Lydia woke up thinking that the dream came from all the years of worry about the safety of the old furnace, so she just dismissed the warning.

As it turned out, no one ever asked Lydia or me how we happened to have all the children out on the field when the explosion took place. Everyone was just so grateful that we were all safe that I guess that it never occurred to anyone to wonder.

"It was a real miracle that no one was in the building when the furnace blew up," they all said for many years to come.

Chapter 10

Healing:
Body, Mind, and Spirit

The essence of healing is the restoring of wholeness. Illness and suffering can create blockages to our full engagement with life, limiting our ability to find the fulfillment for which we incarnated. Life tends to shrink in proportion to the demands of our distress. Though physical ills are the most apparent, we are held back as well by psychological, energetic, and spiritual maladies, which can also wound or stop us as surely as any physical limitation.

Because feelings of being stuck, contracted, or limited are common, we can tell that healing has begun when there is a shift or a breakthrough that creates movement and energy. We may feel that dammed-up energy has been released or that something broken inside has been restored. A transformation has taken place that allows us to move forward again. Healing will mean something quite different for each of us since each life is unique and has its own set of circumstances and imperatives as traveling companions. It will come in a way that is appropriate to the purposes and patterns of our own individual journey.

When healing occurs you know it. Your focus shifts, the release of energy lifts you up, and it is clear that you are on a new path, now facing in a new direction. Whether we are getting over the flu or overcoming a lifetime of suffering, this awareness fills us, body, mind, and spirit, with sweet relief, gratitude, and joy.

Relief from the pain and suffering of illness; the creation of emotional peace; healing of the spirit; transformation—each of these aspects of healing is represented in the stories here. They tell of visitations in which the gift of healing comes unbidden from the afterlife to someone in need.

A common thread in several stories is the fascinating suggestion that healing has come not only to relieve suffering, but also because the illness is preventing the person's full participation in the overarching design of his or her destiny. Some condition is holding that person back from the life she is meant to live, the work he is meant to do. While the limitations of illness, infirmity, and suffering may well be elements of some individual life patterns, it is implied here that in some cases it is necessary to go past the blockage in order to fulfill the vision and potential for which you have taken birth.

In other stories we find healing of emotional wounds, as when a dear friend returns from the afterlife to heal the feelings of jealousy and envy that became a distressing part of the final years of the friendship before her passing. Another loved one from the hereafter, with infinite patience, seeks to start the emotional healing of early sexual abuse while recognizing that healing can be a slow process that must pass through layer after layer of pain, perhaps taking a lifetime to complete.

Healing of the fear or denial of death plays a central role in three of the stories. An inordinate fear of death, so wounding to the heart and soul, can cripple emotionally, holding any of us back from full engagement with life. In one account, a woman speaks about her very vivid, personal terror of death, powerful enough to constrict the scope of her life until her grandmother's visitation lovingly reveals to her that she does not have to go on living in fear.

Another tells of a man who, until a visitation, had little conscious awareness of the fear of death. He confronts in himself this existential fear, which plays some role in all our lives. Unaware of its existence in his psyche until the instant of its healing, he is swept up in the joy of realization, thus finding healing and freedom from an invisible bondage.

Imagine how your own life would be different if your feelings about death were transformed. We each hold our own personal fears; we are all, as well, participants in the age-old, primal, collective fear of death, which we inherit at birth. Every visitation story offers us spiritual medicine to help in the healing of this fear because it reveals every life as an ongoing expression of eternity.

Yet another tells the story of healing, not only for the person still alive on earth, but also for the one who has passed on. A man who died in an accident with his wife and children is being patiently and lovingly protected from the knowledge of his own death so that gentle healing may evolve gradually over time, without a shock to his unprepared mind and heart. Witnessing this afterlife scenario, the writer discovers how she may bring healing into her own life.

Healing of every sort—physical, psychological, energetic, and spiritual—can take place over time or happen in the twinkling of an eye. That our loved ones in the afterlife know of our suffering and care deeply about us and the onward flow of our lives speaks once again of the love, presence, and connection extending beyond the veil of death.

Like being pulled by a magnet toward another direction

Invisible Support

by Howard Lanz

The doctors said that I would likely be in a wheelchair before I was thirty. Diagnosed with a serious congenital spinal problem at eighteen, I found it increasingly difficult to live with the pain, which was my constant companion. Though I went about my life as normally as possible, the pain and weakness in my back were a constant reminder to be careful and to limit my activities.

By the time I was twenty-eight, my life was mostly about pain and limitation. My awareness had shrunk down to the size of the pain, which stayed with me all hours of the day and night and imposed more and more limitations on my activities.

One night I was lying in bed, almost asleep, when I was jolted awake by a noise in the room. Opening my eyes, I saw my uncle standing at the foot of the bed, clearly visible even in the dark room because of the glow that emanated from him, especially around his face.

He was smiling with glee as he began moving slowly toward me. It was then that I saw that he was visible only from about the knees up. Uncle Mort floated up until he was directly over me, and then he spoke, though I don't recall that he moved his mouth at all. I felt a gentle pressure and heat throughout the length of my spine, and he said, "This is not what your life is meant to be about."

While those were his only actual words, I silently received the communication that the spinal problem had understandably become the focus of my energies, and it was taking me away from my reason for being here. After a few minutes my uncle started drawing away, and the pressure left my back, though the heat remained. He communicated to me silently that my back was completely healed.

Uncle Mort moved back to the foot of the bed, gave me a big smile and a little salute, and vanished. I don't remember going to sleep, but the next thing I knew it was morning. When I woke up, I was in more pain than I had ever been in before. In addition to the terrible pain, I was profoundly disappointed because I had believed that the experience with my uncle was real. What seemed like the most extraordinary experience of my entire life now looked like it must have been just a dream.

When I tried to get out of bed the pain was unendurable, so, feeling great despair and resignation, I went back to sleep and woke up a couple of hours later, around ten in the morning. In my sleepy state it took me a minute to register that I had no pain. I'd lived with some degree of pain at all times for over ten years. Cautiously so as not to break the spell, I sat up and, moving very slowly, stood up. Still no pain. Not only was there no pain, but my body was feeling light and energized beyond belief.

I knew then that Uncle Mort had healed my back and that it would stay healed. Never once did I worry that it was temporary. Filled with excitement, I was already moving away from any concern for my back at all. I could feel myself being pulled in another direction, the direction of my real purpose in life, like a magnet was pulling me. I knew that no matter how long it took or where I had to go, I would find my way. I also took great joy in knowing that I had some invisible support.

Where there was fear, a loving presence brings healing and peace

A Circle of Light

by Ann Nelsh-Mays

Twenty-two years ago, as my mother lay dying, she told me the story of my birth.

Mother had had two unsuccessful pregnancies, each ending in miscarriage at around the sixth month. Pregnant for the third time, she was filled with anxiety. Just before her sixth month, as her anxiety grew to near terror, Mother prayed fervently that her baby be carried to term. One afternoon, as she lay down to nap, she found herself very gently encircled by light. Mother said that she fell asleep within the light and awoke an hour later feeling calm and peaceful for the first time in months.

My mother continued to experience the light every day for the next three months, each time feeling the profoundly loving presence permeate and fill her and each time falling into a deep, healing sleep.

At the time of my birth, Mother had her last encounter with the healing, protecting light. It was revealed to her at that time to be my father's mother, Edna, who died while giving birth to her son many years before.

Healing intercession comes with a reminder to be grateful
for those who came before

Remember Your Ancestors

by Bonnie Horrigan

During the winter of 1997–98, 1 was continually ill with a bronchial infection. Never quite well, I had a constant cough that lasted for over four months, and I continued to experience relapses. Then one night in February I had a truly remarkable dream. In the dream my father, who had been dead for several years, came to me.

He put his hand into my chest. A beautiful white and golden light emanated from his hand, and soon the light was filling my chest. He told me, in a clear and precise voice, "Remember your ancestors. All of your ancestors." Then he wished me well and left.

I woke up knowing that I had been healed. My cough was gone, and the bronchial infection was completely cured. As I lay there in awe of the dream and the experience, I began to think of my ancestors as I had never really done before, grateful to all who had come before me. I said a prayer of thanks to my father for coming to visit and for interceding in this world on my behalf.

Emotional healing restores the bond of friendship

A Walk in the Park

by Lore Korbei

We went to school together from our early childhood on, having met when we were very young. She was part of my family, and I was part of hers. Trained in Vienna, we both worked as psychotherapists there.

There was nothing Katsi didn't know about me, and I doubt there was much I didn't know about her. Yet during the last few years of her life, I painfully felt that she was leaving me behind somehow, growing far beyond me in her understanding of life. Envious of her broad rich life with all her friends, I felt somewhat wounded and jealous that I was never able to get enough from her. Then, at age fifty-three, she died.

On the night of what would have been my friend's fifty-fourth birthday, I had a dream.

My doorbell rang in the morning, and there stood Katsi wanting to go for a walk. I knew she was dead. She told me not to worry about anything and just to come along with her, not making a fuss. So off we went, full of high spirits and talking our heads off as usual, each in a hurry to tell the other as much as possible of our lives and all that had happened since her death.

Spring had just begun in Vienna, and she pointed out a wonderful flower bed next to a house, remarking about her continuing joy in the beauty of nature.

My heart sank when we encountered a group of men and women of our age, people we both knew. Jealousy and envy filled me again with deep emotional pain, for I felt that I did not ever get enough of my friend's attention and focus. Here she is, I thought to myself, visiting me from the afterlife, and I am sure that she will talk to these others and waste our short and precious time together.

But instead I was astonished and delighted, for Katsi just greeted them as we passed by. My friend and I continued walking, taking delight in just being together.

I woke up filled with such joy, and I was able to emerge from deep grief and feel just normally sad. In my heart I'd been able to feel and know my friend's true and deep caring for me.

It was enough, and my emotional pain began to heal.

For some, healing is a process that takes time and requires patience

He Waits

by Minuet

My father, dead now eighteen years, sexually abused me for many years when I was a young child.

Recently he has started coming to me from the other side to help me know more clearly what happened those many years ago and to help me heal and accept the truth—things that have been very difficult for me to do on my own.

I know that he comes to me now for my sake, for my healing, and that the question of his redemption is none of my concern. Although I know his visitations are for my healing, still I face the agonizing choice of whether or not to let him back into my life even for this honorable purpose.

My father stands at my door at night and waits for me, and he haunts the therapy room, too. For the first time in my life my father is not intrusive. He follows the divine command to wait, to be patient, not to intrude. This "knowing" that I have—that he is under an injunction to be patient and wait—is deeply important for me, for if I did not have this understanding I would experience my father's visitations merely as intrusive memories of my childhood.

I have learned from this experience that a boundary is not just a concept made up by modern psychologists. Boundaries are created by God to define and protect the human soul, and when they are violated he works indomitably to restore them.

My father waits, respecting my boundaries—my physical, mental, emotional, and spiritual boundaries. It is mine to decide if I want to accept his offering of healing or not.

I do not yet have an ending to my story.

Healing heart and soul

Laughter

by William Mann

There alone by the edge of the sea at my grandfather Sam's house, in my dream I looked out upon the deserted beach, seeing nothing around me but the sea in every direction.

Suddenly I was looking deeply into the eyes and soul of my grandfather Sam, who had been dead nearly ten years. Enlivened and filled with joy and radiant energy, Grandfather looked into my eyes and just laughed. He laughed the most joyful, powerful, clear, full-bellied laugh that I have ever heard in my life. Grandfather's explosion of laughter contained all of eternity.

In a state of pure elation—no words were spoken—he communicated an awesome feeling of ecstasy and, with it, the knowledge that there is nothing to fret about. Nothing at all in the universe to fret about. I could feel my heart and solar plexus tingling and vibrating with energy.

His immense joy is the joy that in time will come to everyone. The absolute knowing that this is what awaits me and those I love filled me with an overwhelming gratitude and peace.

Grandfather's laughter chased all of my fears away, existential fears that I didn't even realize that I'd had about death and the afterlife. Allowed somehow to see into the infinite, I experienced it as a state of passionate joy and release. Grandfather let me see eternity in him, and my soul was healed of the collective darkness that we hold when we do not know of the vast continuation of life. We live our earthly lives as deeply wounded beings when we hold the belief that life and love and passion simply end with the death of the body.

I was there with my own body and soul, lucid and awake. It was a vivid and real dream beyond anything that can be called a dream. My body was asleep, while my soul was totally awake. When I arose from sleep, I knew that it had been a visitation of some sort, that my grandfather came to me, to reach me, to leave me with something that would change the very way I journey through life. I have carried it with me every day, and I can feel Grandfather's healing gift as it lightens this sometimes heavily weighted world.

Release from the fear of death can be the greatest healing of all

Return to God
by Debra Garcia

The day that my grandmother died, a big part of my life ended. The night she returned, an even larger life was given back to me.

In the three months since her passing, I was sick with anguish and grief. Not a day had gone by that hadn't found me immersed in the deepest sadness, my tears sometimes so wrenching that they took my breath away.

My beautiful grandmother came to me one night and changed my way of being in the world, changed and healed my life for the rest of my days. I could see Grandma in the doorway coming toward me, hands together behind her back. Even now I can vividly recall it. She was wearing her green print, ankle-length dress, one of my favorites. She appeared to be twenty years younger and incredibly radiant, her hair in shimmering silver curls. Without a trace of any pain or worry, she exuded only contentment and love.

Although no words were spoken aloud, we communicated deeply through our eyes. Grandmother's loving gaze told me that she was watching over me. Her eyes said not to cry for her anymore. She wanted me to know that she was whole and well, truly alive, deeply happy and at peace.

Grandma knew that I had been deeply wounded by my early years of religious education, that I suffered deeply from my terrible fear and dread of what lay beyond this life. This visitation from the other world, by someone whom I could wholeheartedly trust, opened up a new life to me. My soul experienced the deepest possible transformation the moment I knew that there is a beautiful place waiting for us where we will be reunited with those we love.

A lifetime of fear was healed in me that night.

The healing my grandma blessed me with that night is still present today. Opening up my heart to God and to life, I live with the full assurance that when my time comes to leave this earth, not only will my grandmother be there waiting for me, but also there will be a whole new world in which I will have my next beginning.

Participating in the healing of her departed friend, a woman brings back the insights and commitment to heal her own life

If I Were to Die Today
by Susan Scolastico

Many years ago, my closest friend, Rosemary, her husband, David, and two of her three young children were killed instantly in an automobile accident on their way to visit me. Rosemary and I had known each other for years, and our children, who were the same age, played together frequently. My heart was broken, and I was inconsolable for a very long time.

Rosemary and I had shared deeply held spiritual beliefs about the existence of the soul, life after death, and reincarnation. David was an avowed atheist. Very threatened by her spiritual search and her thirst for knowledge, he believed that there was no afterlife and that when our brain was dead, that was the end. We would no longer exist. David was also depressed much of the time.

One morning, several months after their deaths, as I sat for my customary meditation, all of sudden I felt myself rapidly yet gently floating upward. I floated through the roof, over the house, and into the sky, with earth receding below me. I was fully conscious, being very certain that I was not dreaming. All of a sudden, like Dorothy in *The Wizard of Oz*, I landed in a field of dried wheat grass. Before me stood a familiar-looking house, quite similar to Rosemary and David's house.

I walked onto the porch and peered through the screen door. There was David, sitting in the living room, looking depressed as usual. Nothing seemed to have changed. He glanced up and acknowledged me and did not appear to be surprised at all to see me. I thought to myself, "How shall I relate to him?" knowing that he was dead and I was alive. But clearly, he wasn't aware that he was dead. I just knew that I couldn't blurt out the truth to him. "I'll relate to him in a way that's familiar and comfortable to him," I thought to myself. So I asked him to show me his house and his beloved garden.

David began to lead me through the house and down a hall that had photographs of the family on the wall. As we turned the corner to the kitchen, to my surprise, there were the two children who had been killed, happily playing on the floor. Rosemary was stirring a large pot of spaghetti, David's favorite meal. She looked up and gave me a conspiratorial wink.

In that moment, I knew that she and the children were part of a scenario created for David's healing. Rosemary told me through an unspoken communication that it was a temporary arrangement so that David's spirit could heal as he gradually realized that his body was dead but that he was still alive.

In that instant, I was flooded with a profound vision. I saw earth below me, and I knew with all of my being that one's earthly lifetime is like a blink of an eye, over so quickly. The only things I would take with me when I left earth would be my inner reality, the compassion and love that I had shared, my beliefs, and the knowledge I had gained. After my death I would examine my life to see if I was pleased with the way I lived, and if not, I would want to make it right.

David's strong belief that there is only earthly life and that when his body died he would no longer exist led him to recreate the same experience after death that he had created in life. A strong belief that death would extinguish consciousness kept him from realizing that he had died. It seemed that Rosemary and the children, and even I, were gently helping him to realize the truth that his spirit would outlast his body.

Suddenly, again like Dorothy in Oz, realizing that I was a long way from home, I wondered how I would return. With that thought, I felt myself swooping back to earth and gently reentering my body, filled with love and amazement at what had happened.

I spent the next few hours writing down what was important to me in my own life, asking myself, "If I were to die today, what would I take with me?" My first thought was that I would regret that I had not spent more time with my children. I did not want to die and have regrets about something I could have remedied in life. I decided to take action right away.

My two daughters and my son had been living with their father because I was too busy in my career to give them the attention they needed. I realized now that I would not take my career with me through the door of death but I would take the love that I had shared with my children—love that was not just felt but acted upon. I immediately quit my job, took one that gave me control of my own time, and brought my daughters to live with me.

In that mystical and transforming experience, both David and I found spiritual healing as well as the healing and reorienting of values and ideals. Each day I ask myself, "If I were to die today, what would I take with me?" If my answer is that I would take anger, regret, depression, or negativity of some kind, then I do my best to make changes in my life so that I am living up to my highest spiritual ideals and values.

Chapter 11

Evidential Visitations:
The Unknown Made Known

Everyone loves to hear the fascinating stories of visitations in which something is revealed that was not known before or an event is foretold that later comes to pass just as predicted. Though validation isn't needed, still we find it thrilling when something occurs that cannot be explained by any other means. It tends to confirm what we may already believe or have experienced subjectively in our hearts.

The stories in this chapter tell of such foretelling and evidential experiences. Each brings information that has come from a higher vantage point or a perspective other than our own. While some predict the future and others give verifiable information, many stories combine both of these aspects. In my own story, "Sweet William," the future is foretold and verifiable information is given that did not come to me through regular channels. Interestingly, I was not in any emotional or physical need at the time of William's visit. So many visitations come to comfort, to reassure, to protect, to help the person in a time of need, and it is interesting to find that sometimes no apparent need is being met. This visitation came to me, well, out of the blue.

Some visitations occur just before the need is known, as in two stories in which emotionally demanding events took place, both preceded by visitations that provided the help and support needed to face them. These caring visitations brought assurance of a kind that could come in no other way.

In another story a frightened young woman is in a state of profound physical, mental, and emotional distress while on a journey across the Atlantic. She is in great need but has no reason to imagine that assistance will come as it did, from a stranger who, possessing not only wisdom but specific knowledge of the future, gives her the courage to change her life forever.

Another woman, completely unaware that she is being cheated in a financial agreement, receives this vital information and is able to confront the situation and restore the money due her. And finally, a young man's conscious spiritual journey begins after the tragic death of his brother, when, in a visitation, he is shown something about the accident not known to anyone at the time, something that is validated weeks later.

While evidential visitations are fascinating and wonderfully confirming, for some of us they may bring up more questions than they answer, questions about the nature of reality itself, the nature of time, and issues of free will and destiny, cause and effect. Having my mother's accidental death foretold left me haunted by such questions for a very long time as I deeply pondered the vast implications. What does it mean that someone in the afterlife could know, in advance, of an accident? How can that be? Every assumption ever held about the nature of existence is thrown into question, as these experiences powerfully suggest that things are not necessarily the way we have been taught to believe.

What is this enigmatic life we live? Each of us, in our own time and in our own way, must investigate the great mysteries of existence, knowing only that there are no easy answers, just lots of evocative clues. Few experiences will throw you out of your intellect and into the deep waters of mystery and enchantment as thoroughly as an evidential visitation.

Revealing the past and the future and bringing an unusual gift

Sweet William

by Lee Lawson

It was only our second date. Martin and I were sitting quietly on his front porch looking at the stars when suddenly I became aware of a presence other than my own—in my mind. I realized that it was someone distinctly not me. Since it came to me so gently and so lovingly, I felt no fear, no anxiety, just the awareness of another presence. This one was different from most of my previous visitation experiences, in that I did not immediately know who was trying to get my attention. "Who are you?" I asked silently.

The presence introduced himself as William, saying that he was Martin's father, who had died many years earlier when Martin was a very young child. He went on to tell me many things about his beloved son, including that Martin's purpose in the world was to be a "force of love." I was quite surprised when he said that Martin and I would marry someday. This was only our second date!

Preparing to go, William asked me if I would give Martin a gift from him. When I expressed my confusion about how such a thing might happen, he reassured me saying, "I want you to tell him of our visit and then give him an image from me. Give him the image of a toy fire engine and a fireman's hat."

With that, we parted. I sat there stunned. I knew nothing whatsoever about Martin's past and little enough about his present. Was his father dead? Was he named William? I'm supposed to tell this man, whom I barely know, that I have just been having a chat with his dead father, William, and that he sent along a gift? "And, by the way, he said that you are a 'force of love'—and my future husband!"

Sitting silently for several minutes, I debated about telling Martin what had just happened. He would understandably think me a complete lunatic, and that would be that. End of story.

Finally, and only because of the compelling power of the experience itself, I decided to get it over with and tell Martin everything.

(Almost everything. I did not mention the part about our being married someday.)

Martin sat perfectly still as I talked. He did not move a muscle. When I got to the part about "and he asked me to give you a gift," I gave Martin the image of the toy fireman's hat and truck. Tears shot out of his eyes and he began to cry softly. A minute later, without saying a word, he walked inside and came back with a photograph of himself at age four. In the photo he is wearing a fireman's hat and sitting next to a little fire engine, gifts from his father, William, shortly before he died.

Martin and I did marry two years later and have been married for fifteen years. Over the years I have had other visitations from William. Some of them I think of as love notes, just lovingly saying hello. At other times he comes to help in the confusion and pain that are some part of every marriage.

Always William's presence leads to greater understanding and greater love. And, simply, it is wonderful to know that he is there, loving us.

Convincing evidence that their reunion really happened

A Journey Without End

by Stephen Lange

Our whole family was especially proud of this handsome young man who looked so good in his uniform and had such a rich, promising life ahead of him. My brother, Tom, was a navy pilot. He and his wife were expecting their first child when he was killed in a plane crash.

Coming less than a month before my eighteenth birthday, Tom's accident shook the solid, secure world of my childhood to its core.

The fateful day of the crash, August 7, is forever burned into my memory. I was at my work as a bag boy at the grocery store when my father arrived to pick me up. Choking out the news of the crash, he sat there in the car crying, something I had never seen him do before. The enchanted world of my childhood had been shattered forever.

Emotionally exhausted, I went to my upstairs bedroom that night anticipating being awake all night as I wrestled with the heart-wrenching questions, Why? Why Tom? Why now?

Eventually, dropping off into a fitful slumber, I slept for a couple of hours before I was awakened by the lights in the room being turned on. There, at the foot of my bed, stood my dead brother, Tom.

Some part of my brain knew that he was dead and shouldn't be there—and if he was, shouldn't I be afraid? But there was no fear, and I exclaimed, "Tom! You're alive!"

I jumped up and tried to hug him, but he motioned to me not to touch him. As he sat on the side of the bed, I pulled up a chair and we began to talk. Tom answered many of my questions and soothed my grieving heart, constantly reassuring me that he was all right. He promised me that everything would be okay.

The only thing I noticed about him that seemed unusual was a small cut about an inch long above his left eye. I didn't speak of it but only made a mental note. Finally Tom said it was time for him to go but that I was not to worry, as he would be around whenever I needed him. Then he disappeared.

When Tom was gone, I was shaken enough that I went back to bed leaving the light on. The peace of mind he had given me returned shortly, and I dropped off quickly into peaceful sleep.

I thought constantly about what had happened, both the next morning and for many days afterward. Telling no one at the time, I didn't know if anyone would believe me, and I was beginning to wonder myself if it had all been just a very dramatic dream.

Two weeks after the funeral, Tom's widow sent the family a long letter detailing the results of the navy investigation into the crash.

Due to the nature of the incident, it said, my brother had been thrown clear of the craft and had died instantly of internal injuries. The only outward evidence whatsoever of the injury to his body was a small, one-inch cut above his left eye—exactly as I had seen it the night that Tom came to me.

As my mother read the letter aloud, I received the confirmation I needed to know that his spirit had indeed visited me that terrible night. I was greatly excited by this proof that death was not the end of existence.

Six weeks after Tom's death my mother died of an aneurysm. I believe that she died of a broken heart. A few days later, at her funeral service, I saw my brother, Tom, holding my sleeping mother in his arms as he reassured us that she would get a long, much-needed rest. He would be there with her when she awoke.

Thus began my ongoing journey into the heart of life, as I was compelled to reevaluate everything I thought I knew about the world and my place in it.

An epic story of the intricate web of connection in our lives

The Darkest Night

by Ida Levine

For you to understand the story, I have to tell it to you from the beginning.

I grew up in Budapest. It was my mother and me. My father, a lens grinder, died when I was just five years old. Though very poor, we always had a place to live and food to eat, but we barely scraped by. My mother was a seamstress, but she was often sick.

When I was fifteen I left school to find work. My mother was very disappointed. She knew that I needed to have skills and at least a little bit of education to get by in the world. I needed to find work, but of course there wasn't any to be had during those years. Things were getting harder for everyone, and Hitler was starting to cause more and more trouble for all of us Jews. Many people were out of work, even a lot of the men. That's how bad it was.

We were living with Aunt Elena at that time, but she, too, was very poor and barely able to live, much less take on the burden of keeping me and Mama. It seemed so hopeless.

Every night Mama cried, and day by day her health was getting worse. Everyone was afraid in those days. "What will become of us?" is all we talked about, all we thought about, day after day.

My aunt came home one night telling us that her friend's daughter went on a boat to America, New York, where she got work sewing in a factory. There was an arrangement you could make with the shipping company, her friend told her. You gave a little money now, and out of your wages they would take the rest, leaving you enough to live on.

My mother became more and more excited, asking her to tell us again every detail. A terrible fear came into my heart when finally I understood: she was thinking this would be something for me—a way out for me!

My mother insisted there was no other choice. She said I had to go, to save myself. To have some hope of a better life out of poverty. She would stay there with her sister for now, and later she would come to me in America.

But, she said, I had to go now. I cried and begged her to let me stay, but back then you did what your mother said no matter if you liked it or not.

Mama and Aunt Elena went right away to every relative and friend in Budapest to bring together the bits of money they could for my trip. So young then, I didn't realize at the time what the adults knew—that the Hitler trouble would get much worse. It was already getting more dangerous every day. They wanted to get me out before it was too late.

Two months later, after a long, exhausting train trip from Budapest, I boarded the boat at Marseilles and was herded, with all the others, into the steerage deck down below. It was an awful place with hundreds of strangers, and it was the first time in my life I had been away from my mother.

I was certain I would never see her again. America, to me, was like a monster waiting for me across the ocean with a big, open mouth.

I was shaking on that boat, I was so scared. In black despair, I couldn't take in all of what was happening to me. Three days out from Europe, the storms were so bad that we all became seasick. I have never in my life been so miserable as those first days out at sea. I began to think that I would rather be dead, that I could not stand the loneliness and fear for another day. Right back to Budapest I would go; I would not even get off the boat. I would do anything, but I would not go to America no matter what happened to me.

We were out six days when the terrible storm finally stopped. It was the middle of the night, and I managed to get myself up and go out into the stairwell, where I sat down and started to cry again. It was the darkest night of my life.

I was so afraid and exhausted that I didn't know what to do. When I looked up, right in front of me was a woman looking down at me, asking if I needed some help. No one had said a single kind word to me in all the days since I had left Budapest, so when she said that to me, well, I just started to cry some more. She sat down and put her arms around me and held on to me while I cried and cried. I could not even say anything to her for the longest time.

And then I told her everything from the beginning—about my father dying, about not having a home, about seeing Mama getting sicker and sicker, about being out in the world all by myself, about planning to go back to Budapest. Even about wanting to die. I told her everything.

She listened to me without saying anything until I finished the whole story. Then she started telling me things, things about my own life—you know, what my life would be like in America.

Miriam—that was her name—told me that I would marry a boy called Rubin. We would meet in New York. We would marry and then, later, move to Canada. (I had never even heard of Canada; I thought it must be part of New York.) Rubin and I would have a good life together, she said, not maybe an always-easy life, but a good one. We would be a family—three children, Miriam said, a boy and two girls, and grandchildren even. She said all these things would happen for me.

I got to know all about my life and how things would work out okay for me. Miriam said that I had to go ahead, looking forward, not backward, if I was to have this better life for myself. She said that I had to be brave because there would be other times when I might feel afraid. (When I think of how young I was then! I was just a child.)

All night we talked. Miriam looked to me to be about forty-five years, with such red hair all piled up. She wore a long blue dress and had on a little brooch made of tiny sparkling diamonds in the shape of a rose. I was looking at the brooch because I had never seen such a beautiful thing as this before.

She told me that her husband gave it to her for their wedding anniversary and that I would one day have such a brooch. That brought me near to crying again because I did not even have money to buy food. Never would I, myself, have anything like that rose brooch.

Just a little bit of light was coming on the horizon when Miriam stood up to leave. I begged her to stay with me. But when I reached my hand up to grab her arm, she disappeared. Just vanished under my hand! In my life before or since I was never so surprised by anything.

The rest of the time on the boat after that, I was able to start looking ahead a little more, to make some plans for myself. Oh, I was still anxious, but not so afraid. I could feel Miriam with me. Sometimes I could feel her at night and even hear her whisper in my ear, but I never did see her again. I didn't know what to make of it, how she was there one minute and then vanished into thin air.

There was this tiny bit of hope in me that I would be all right. She gave me just enough courage and hope to go on with my life.

Now, to make a long story short, I did go to work along with hundreds of others in the garment district of New York. Jewish immigrants like myself. The following year I met Rubin, and we married in the spring. I was eighteen by then, and our first two babies were born in the next three years, the boy and the first girl. Right after the second baby, Rubin wanted to move back to Toronto, where he had grown up. His father, a widower, lived there.

The first time we went to see his father there in Toronto—I'll never forget this as long as I live—I had just walked through the front door into the apartment and, even before I could say hello to my father-in law, I saw her picture on the wall. Miriam! The woman on the ship! I was speechless. There she was, the beautiful red hair all piled up, sitting there in the same blue dress. And of course, there was the little rose brooch, with all of the tiny sparkly little diamonds.

Tears poured out of my eyes. Everything came back to me. My husband and his father didn't know why I was crying. They sat me down, and Rubin just held onto me until I was okay again. I couldn't help it. I told them everything—how she stayed with me through that terrible night and helped me go on to New York and how the things she told me came true, just like she said they would.

The real reason I was crying—and I couldn't even say this at the time—was that when I saw the picture and who she was, that she was my Rubin's own mother, and when I knew that what she said was true, well, I just felt that my life was—well, protected. It is so hard to use the right words. We were being watched over. Do you know what I'm trying to say? And that made me cry more than anything. It is very hard for me to explain.

My father-in-law then took a small wrapped package out of his pocket and handed it to me. The little card said, "Welcome, Daughter Ida."

He said to me, "Before my wife died twelve years ago, she asked me to save this for Rubin's own wife someday. It's for you."

Of course you know that inside the little package was the rose brooch she had on, with the little diamonds. My father-in-law told me about how everyone called her Rosie when she was alive because of this beautiful red hair she had, so he gave her this brooch made into a rose. It was for their wedding anniversary a long time ago, before she died.

That is so many years ago now. We've had a good life, Rubin and me and the children. Not without our troubles, like anyone else, but always a family. Rubin, like all the men, had to go to the war, but he came back. And he's done okay for himself. Always we've had enough. The children have their own children now, and there are five great-grandchildren.

My dear mother, God bless her, survived Hitler and the war in

Europe, and we brought her here to Toronto. Until she died, she lived with us. And I thought I was never going to see her again.

What would have happened to me if Rubin's mother had not come to me when she did? I don't know. I just don't know how things would have been for me. How things would have turned out. Not like this. That much I do know.

And one more thing—our second daughter we named Miriam Rose.

The unknown made known just in time

Inside Information
by Eva Pagano

My husband and I were getting a divorce. Because we'd both really poured ourselves into building our art gallery over the course of our fourteen-year marriage, it wasn't easy to settle the money and property issues. That task finally accomplished, we were ready to sign the papers that would finalize the agreements. The process had been a reasonably friendly one as divorces go. We both felt that a fair settlement had been reached and were relieved that it was finally to be finished. I was eager to return to my native Italy. It was time to move on.

The night before the signing I couldn't sleep and finally got up when I saw that I'd apparently left the light on in the living room. As I came into the room I was enveloped by a golden light that sent waves of electricity through me, little shocks that didn't hurt. There was my uncle sitting calmly in the rocker, smiling, it seemed to me, with obvious delight at being there.

As I went forward to embrace him, he motioned me away and toward the sofa, where I sat down. My Uncle Vito told me how my husband had been taking money out of the gallery for over ten years and that it was all in a secret bank account. He told me the exact amount, $167,000. I was stunned. I'd trusted my husband completely with the gallery money and never suspected that he was even capable of keeping such a secret from me. Nonetheless, I trusted my uncle more and knew with absolute certainty that what he said was true.

Uncle Vito and I sat together for a few minutes before he gradually disappeared, along with the golden light that filled the room.

The next morning outside the lawyer's office, before we went in for the meeting, I confronted my husband with my knowledge of a secret account containing $167,000. I think it was such shock to him that I knew about the bank account and exactly how much was in it that without any hesitation at all he confessed that it was true. He had the money. He'd kept it a secret, and no one else in the world knew of its existence.

We did get things worked out, and I eventually forgave him for his deception. Of course, he was dying to know how I found out about the money, which he had gone to such ingenious and extraordinary lengths to keep such a secret for so many years. My one little bit of revenge was that I never told him how I knew. And it drove him nuts.

During life's most difficult passage, someone is there to help us across

The Crossing

by Lee Lawson

As I sat at my easel, deeply immersed in painting, I suddenly became aware of a brilliant energy filling the room. The entire room was shimmering and glowing with love, with presence and life. Without a split second's hesitation I knew that it was my father, who had died twenty years before.

Every molecule in the room and every cell of my being were filled with Father's presence. For a long, long time not a word was spoken, not a thought passed through my mind. Then I asked, "What are you doing here?"

"I have come to help your mother," my father replied very simply. Those were the only words spoken during the entire visitation.

So blissful was I now that it never even occurred to me to ask why Mother needed help. The captivating joy of our being together filled me until the experience ended.

Overflowing, I raced out of the studio to tell Martin what had happened, how wonderful it had been to be with my father. Even as I told him what my father said about coming to help Mother, I didn't think to wonder what that might mean. I was too happy to think.

At sixty-four, my mother was doing very well, was healthier than anyone I knew, and had the energy of a six-year-old. She didn't need any help.

The next morning Mother was in a car accident, which caused her death. As she was coming home from the corner store where she had bought strawberries for lunch guests, while she was waiting to turn at an intersection, an eighteen-year-old girl ran the red light and collided with Mother's car. The girl told the police that she was in a hurry.

My father came to help my mother across. By coming to me the night before, he told me that he would be there with her, that he had come for her so that she would not make that passage alone.

Chapter 12

Making Peace:
Forgiveness and Reconciliation

One of the greatest of all spiritual practices is forgiveness—so antithetical to human nature, so difficult, and so confusing. We are so reluctant to apologize and ask for forgiveness and so unwilling to forgive. Yet nothing will open the heart and soul to the blessings of love as will forgiveness.

Resentment, grievance, and judgment can be carried throughout a lifetime, as can the guilt or rationalization from being blamed, rightly or wrongly, for a transgression. Regardless of who did what to whom, both people in a conflict have accepted the burden of pain and blocking of life force that always accompanies bitterness and separation.

Betrayals of every sort can be the source of estrangement between people who once loved and cared very much for each other—parents and children, husbands and wives, brothers and sisters, friends, neighbors, and associates. Violations both trivial and monumental, lack of kindness, neglect, abuse, and abandonment all can cause hurts that grow over time into deep-seated rancor.

Estrangement that still exists when someone important in our lives dies can cause tremendous ongoing pain and suffering, for, to all appearances, death ends forever the possibility of reconciliation.

When death comes, pain and regret can deepen, and you may feel that surely healing will never and can never come. That which you need so much to say now can never be said. That which your heart longs to hear will never be voiced.

So common is it to hear of suffering caused by this lack of closure, this lost opportunity, that most of us can deeply appreciate stories of visitations in which forgiveness and reconciliation are the focus of the reunion. I have selected several types of stories on this theme. First are stories in which someone from the hereafter returns to ask for forgiveness. Second are stories in which the writer is the one needing to be forgiven by someone who passed on. And, last, we have a reconciliation that could take place only after a father, returning from the afterlife after over two decades, revealed the true story behind the years his son spent in bitterness and hatred.

Creating peace where there has been no peace, reaching out to apologize and ask for forgiveness, accepting an apology and granting forgiveness—all clearly reveal that one is functioning from a new and higher perspective. It is a perspective that comes from the vantage point of eternity.

The spiritual principle of forgiveness is beyond concepts of right and wrong, and it is so contrary to human justice and human nature that it seems impossible. Those who go within to find the wisdom and strength to forgive understand why it is spiritually necessary: it provides unsurpassed healing and blessing.

It is never too late to forgive.

No longer haunted by the past

Healing the Past

by Serena Poisson

My husband was out to sea with his navy helicopter squadron, and the children were away. I was alone that day for a change, enjoying some unusual solitude, when I felt a powerful urge to go outside. Walking out into the yard, I could see the late afternoon sun still high in the western sky. The shadows were just beginning to lengthen. It was then that I saw him.

My first husband, Jim, stood there on the sidewalk opposite the driveway. Jim had died in 1974 at the age of forty-one from the complications of years of alcohol consumption. I had no doubt whatsoever about who it was. He stood with his head tilted just the way he had always stood, and I would have recognized him anywhere. He was wearing a white shirt and dark trousers. Here in the afternoon it was light enough to see his features clearly. Oddly, there was a glow emanating from him, reminding me at the time of how someone glows under black light.

My reaction was strong and immediate. I was terribly afraid of him.

A violent alcoholic, Jim had been physically abusive to the older children and me when he was alive. Terrified, I turned and ran back into the house, slammed the door, and locked it. In that moment, I learned that fear has a taste, metallic and strong. My heart was pounding in my chest, beating so hard I could hear it.

Once inside, the reality and, of course, the absurdity of my actions hit me. A locked door had never kept him out when he was alive, and it certainly wouldn't now. I opened the door and went back outside. Jim was gone. Greatly relieved, I mentioned my experience to no one.

A few mornings later my husband was in the bathroom getting ready for work as I lay in bed slowly waking into the day. Suddenly I felt someone sit on the mattress next to me. Once again fear shot through me, because I knew instantly that it was Jim.

I tried to speak but couldn't make a sound. Then, all at once, I felt myself relax as profound love and gentleness poured through me, filling my heart and mind.

Jim touched my left elbow. It was a caress filled with apology, love, and great warmth. How long the moment lasted, I don't know. Relaxing into it, I felt waves of healing and love wash over me again and again, cleansing me of the tremendous fear and bitterness of our past.

All of the bad memories receded, and the good ones resurfaced. Remembering when I fell in love with Jim so many years before, I recalled the excitement we shared in the birth of our children and the hopes we had for our future. That our love was overshadowed by Jim's alcoholism and everything that goes with it remains a reality, but because of these precious moments, I know now that both of our hearts have healed and we can go on with our lives.

My present husband and I have been together now for thirty-one years. We've been able to work through the many ups and downs that have been a part of our marriage partly because of the forgiveness and reconciliation that took place that day. There is no longer a ghost from my first marriage that needs to be exorcised. Jim's visit twenty years ago healed and freed my emotions so that, not being haunted by the past, I could devote my whole heart to this marriage and my children and my work.

Ultimately, only one thing matters

Only Love

by Harley Moor

My father was a hellfire-and-brimstone preacher in the small town where I grew up. As I started to see his religious ranting as garbage, I saw how he had dominated my life with all of his rules and regulations from God Almighty. He hated anyone who disagreed with him and damned them to hell.

When I was a teenager we started arguing about religion (and everything else), and for the rest of the time that I lived in my parents' house my father and I were almost constantly screaming and cursing each other. When I was a senior in high school I became a raving atheist. We were really at each other all the time. Finally, he threw me out of the house and disowned me, damning me to eternal hell. We despised each other passionately.

I went away to college, overjoyed to be gone and fully intending never to go back. Three years later, I did go back, for his funeral. I didn't want to go even then, but I went to help my mother settle things. In truth, I was glad he was gone.

A few nights after the funeral, while sorting through some of his stuff, I thought I heard someone laugh. I stopped, listened intently, and heard it again, only this time it was right there in the room. I turned around and saw my father sitting there, in his favorite chair, laughing his head off. I realized then that I had never before, in my entire life, ever heard the man laugh. Not once.

"What is so funny?" I demanded.

I will never forget it. "We were both wrong!" he said and howled with laughter. A bolt, just like lightning, shot out of him into me. It was a bolt of pure love. When that happened I had perfect understanding that he was saying that love is the only thing that matters. Nothing else. Absolutely nothing else.

For weeks afterward I felt his searing love shooting through me. At the same time, I was filled with sickening grief and regret that we had wasted our precious time together when he was alive. It took me a few years to come to peace with that.

A lifetime of pain and bitterness dissolves into unconditional love

The Healing Heart
by Cheryl Fuller

I watched as the urn containing my mother's ashes was placed alongside those of her husband and two-year-old son.

Two weeks after her death, my mother was standing just a few feet in front of me, radiant and filled with a joyful contentment I'd never seen in her when she was alive. A brilliant light surrounded her body. She appeared to be in her early twenties, young and beautiful. Her hair was the natural blond color of her youth, before the silver-gray clouds of loss and sorrow swept across her life.

As we embarked on a journey together, my mother reached out to me, her arms wide open with pure love. Her love permeated the air around us with a sweet fragrance of flowers. Hesitant at first, frozen in a moment of our bitter past, I could not help remembering that when she was alive, her conditional affection, tangled up with critical, abusive words, had wounded me painfully and left deep and painful scars.

Even as I wondered if I would be safe responding to her embrace, I had no doubt about the hunger in my heart. Since the age of eight I had longed for her closeness, for my mother's love. It seemed just seconds before my reluctance melted, and suddenly, I had no more need to protect myself or anxiously hold back out of fear. With a new trust and understanding emerging between us in that timeless moment, I felt total peace in my emotions. Peace was a freedom I'd so seldom experienced with her when she was alive.

The next sensation I felt was indescribable, as her arms surrounded me in an embrace filled with the most exquisite, unconditional love I have ever felt from another person. Instantly, her love incinerated years of emotional pain, anger, and fear like a fire clearing deadwood from land soon to be planted with spring flowers. Saturating every cell of my being was my mother's love, unconditionally.

In our embrace of forgiveness, there healed a lifetime of critical words and my childhood terror of abandonment. My mother and I were one, merged into love. Nothing mattered except being in that embrace. I was consumed in infinite love, the kind of love that lifts the sun in the morning and makes it shine and ignites the stars at night into brilliance.

In returning to me after her death, my mother gave me the greatest gift a person can receive in any realm. She gave me the opportunity to forgive her after so many difficult years between us. Only in forgiveness can I move away from the wounding and pain that consumed my life.

Where once there was a tangle of deadwood, now wildflowers grow.

Through the last barrier of fear and resistance to forgiveness and healing

A Beginning
by Lyn Lavel

Relief swept through me when I heard the news of my father's death. He had sexually abused me in my childhood, and the violation remained unacknowledged by my family all these years.

For several hours after Mother's call, I felt a presence there with me, one that I studiously avoided by keeping busy with preparations for the trip to Mother's house. But it was relentless, and finally, with no other choice, I let go, turned my attention toward the presence, and, not surprisingly, found that it was my father.

A great healing began to take place in me that day as my father acknowledged his violation and expressed his deepest sorrow over the pain he had caused me. It was his hope that I would ultimately be able to fully forgive him. And I was able to ask for and receive my father's forgiveness for my arrogance toward him throughout my adult life.

Every day for two weeks my father was there with me, ecstatic while telling me that he never before felt so good or experienced such deep peace. Laughing joyfully, he urged me not to be sad for him.

In the days following his death I was somehow able to discern the progress and movement of Father's healing and renewal, until after a time, words ceased and we communicated solely through images.

One key image that he showed me each day: he was walking along a stream, appearing younger and younger, more whole, more alive with every passing day. Others were present with my father to support his healing and progress. After a few weeks, the experience gradually faded and he was not there with me in the same direct way.

Continuing my own intensive inner work, I began healing from the childhood incest. I discovered that forgiveness is a process.

Though it can happen in an instant, it sometimes comes quite gradually, over time.

About two years ago, once again my father came to me, his presence, energy, and soul now much clearer and filled with light. Because each of us had done so much healing of the bitterness and hurt between us, Father asked me if I could fully forgive him now, fully accept the love that he had for me.

Even though tremendous healing had taken place in me, I was surprised to find that I was still hesitant about surrendering and opening to someone who had hurt me so. Through grace alone, I was able to break through that last barrier of fear and resistance and open my heart to receive my father with love and to experience the profound transformation of forgiveness.

Given another chance to express love and appreciation

From Darkness into Light

by Roger Glass

Shock seared my belly like a hot knife. I was stunned when they told me that Mother had died in an automobile accident. It couldn't be true! A rush of intense emotion poured through my mind and into my body the way lightning splits the sky on a stormy night. Disbelief, despair, guilt, and helplessness threatened to drag me deeper and deeper into the darkness.

I couldn't believe that she was really gone, and I despaired that I would never be able to talk to her again. I could never tell her now that I was sorry—sorry I had not told her how much I really loved her. Sorry because I could have been nicer and kinder to her. Sorry that I had not treated my mother with the respect she deserved. I felt so helpless that I could do nothing to change it. Nothing. There wasn't a thing I could change.

This was the darkest time in my life, my dark night of the soul. I cried until there were no tears left.

Sometime later, Mother came to my wife in a dream saying, "Tell Roger to open his mind." Then I, too, had a dream:

Facing in my direction, Mother was standing in front of a landscape so beautiful that there are no earthly words to describe it. She was talking with a man who had his back to me, whose hair was almost too white to look at. I knew that this being was God. Mother was looking directly at him, and I could see her face over his left shoulder.

As I took one or two steps toward them, God moved back a step and to the left so that I could pass, putting me face-to-face with my mother. By simply turning to the left I would be able to see the face of God, but somehow I knew that I should not look directly at him. My eyes stayed intently on Mother.

"Well, hello there, son!" A joyous smile filled my mother's radiant face.

Her eyes shone with an incredibly beautiful, ethereal light. She was happy. Earthly problems were no longer important because her focus was now in another, higher place.

Surrounding me was love so wonderful, so pure, that it defies every description. There are no words in the human language that can speak of the warmth, the security, the gentleness that enveloped me, wrapped around me like a cocoon, engulfing me in its wonder and blessing.

"Mother, I miss you. I love you, and I'm sorry," I said, asking her to forgive me.

My dear mother forgave me for my every transgression and assured me that she would always love me with this same wonderful, all-encompassing love. It is love that I will never forget.

I am certain now that Mother is completely happy and in a wonderful place. That knowledge, along with the certainty of her love and forgiveness, allows me to move forward with my own life to experience the joy we all are seeking.

And I know that one day I will fully understand the wonderful smile on her face.

Looking through the eyes of compassion

Reflection

by Terrie Coffey

Struck and killed by lightning—my brother was dead. My mother's call with this news of Richard plunged me into hysterical screaming and crying. I was inconsolable, overcome by guilt.

From the day he was born with a congenital hip deformity I'd had nothing but hatred for Richard. My mother had to carry him everywhere. Caring for him consumed her time, love, and attention and left nothing for me, just a tiny three-year-old when he was born. Later I had to care for him as well. I saw Richard's physical condition as a tyrant and thief ruling our lives.

Even though he was eventually healed and was finally able to walk by himself, it appeared to me that my mother continued to favor Richard in all things, and I deeply resented him and took every opportunity to exhibit that resentment. Upon learning of his death, I became overwrought with self-hatred and loathing for the years and years of terrible emotional abuse I had dealt him.

The day after Richard's accident, as I was sobbing hysterically into my pillow, I suddenly heard his voice. "Everything is okay," Richard said to me. "In my heart is only love and forgiveness for you."

Startled, I turned toward his voice, and there stood Richard at the foot of my bed, comforting me, telling me not to worry, that he understood why I'd behaved the way I had and that he forgave me. With that, he was gone.

In the wake of Richard's visit I was filled with his love and peace. Until that time I had never reflected on why I'd behaved cruelly and abusively toward him all those years. I suddenly came face-to-face with myself as a tiny three-year-old little girl who felt desperately scared, unloved, alone, and set aside.

Because Richard forgave me, I was able to look upon myself and my actions with compassion and to begin to forgive myself. Both the adult woman and the tiny three-year-old girl found healing that day.

*Understanding brings forgiveness; forgiveness brings spiritual
and emotional rebirth*

Hatred

by Gabe Pricherd

It changes you when you don't have a father anymore because he left you. When all the other kids have a father and you are the only one who doesn't, you feel like there's something wrong with you and your sister and your mother. He left, not because he died and couldn't help it, but because he walked away. He left on purpose because he never wanted to see you again.

I hated him. I hated him because he left. I hated him because it made everybody think that there must be something wrong with us. Why else would a father leave and never come back?

Mama hated him, and so did Sara, and so did I. We hated him every day of every week of the year. It held us together like glue, hating him.

I hated him because I couldn't remember him. I was four when he left, and I couldn't remember his face or the sound of his voice or his eyes or going anyplace together. I had to hate someone I couldn't even remember.

At least Sara remembered him. She was seven. She remembered that she loved him before she hated him. And she remembered the day he didn't come home and the fruitless phone call to the police. And Mama crying. And then Mama angry.

We were ruined. The rest of our lives destroyed because of what he did to us. On purpose. Just left us to rot. That bastard, she used to say. That bastard.

Year after year we got by. We kept to ourselves. Mama didn't have friends, and Sara and I never brought anybody home. We were disgraced. So we had to be more than good, more good than other people. We had to go to church twice a week instead of once. We had to sit through two boring church sermons because he left us. We had to make A's in school because he left us. Everything we did was done with hatred for him, because everything we did, we did because he was gone. Our lives were hard because he went away and never looked back. She said he never looked back. Your father.

We fed our hatred and watched it grow. My mother became the hatred. There wasn't much else to her after a while. They'd had an argument one night, and he'd left the house in a fit. My father had never looked back. He put her through hell. He deserted her. He deserted us. The bastard. Left us to rot.

A lonely and bitter child, I became a lonely, bitter, and miserable young man.

I was in graduate school when Mama died. Sara and I had her buried next to her mother and father. She didn't have any friends. We knew it was his fault, just as everything else was. It took him twenty years to do it, but he put her in an early grave. He left us, and now he took Mama away from us, too.

Two weeks after Mama died I went out to the lake north of town. I couldn't go there when she was alive because he had proposed to her by that lake, so she didn't want Sara or me going there.

Nobody was at the lake. I walked for a few minutes then sat down on the dock. I wanted to be alone.

My eyes closed just for a minute, and when I opened them there was a man sitting on the dock next to me. I didn't hear him come up. He was sitting beside me, close, like he knew me. Like I'd asked him to sit down. I stood up to go someplace else to be alone. Without looking up, he said, "Why don't you stay, Gabe? I'd like to talk to you."

"Do I know you? How do you know my name?"

"I just want to talk to you," the man said. "Do you recognize me? Don't you know who I am?"

"No," I said. "Should I? Who are you?"

"For goodness' sake, Gabe. I'm your father."

I looked at him and knew that it was true, even though he seemed not much older than me. I could see in his eyes that it was true.

"You bastard!" I cried. "Fine time you pick to come back! She's dead. Mama is dead, and Sara and I are grown up, and here you are. What do you want? It's too late. About twenty years too late. You ruined my life. You ruined Sara's life, and you killed Mama. What more do you want? You left us, and now you come back. That's just great." I was jumping around and shouting at him. He didn't move. I yelled. I cursed. I ranted.

"Are you finished?" he asked quietly. "Sit down. I want to tell you something."

I sat down.

"Listen to me, son. I was out of work. Things were hard, and your mother was upset. She was afraid of what would happen to us when the money ran out. I looked for work every day. It was hard paying the rent and keeping food on the table. I came home every day with nothing. We'd already sold everything worth selling, and we even borrowed money from her sister.

"Well, that night she laid into me before I even got through the door. 'You're a good-for-nothing. I should never have married you. My mother told me not to marry you. Don't you know we have two children to feed? What are you going to do? Just tell me, what are you going to do? For God's sake, do something! Do something! Don't you care anything about these children? If you had any—'

"I knew better than anyone that there was no food, no money, no work. You and Sara crying, her screaming, blaming me. I just lost it. I stormed out of the house.

"Your mother didn't need to tell me that I had to do something. I got over to the highway and hitched a ride out of town. I had already decided that morning to go over to Colorado to work the big dam project. They were building these dams over there and hiring men by the thousands. I came home that day to tell her that I was going to get work out in Colorado, but she was yelling at me before I could open my mouth.

"'I'll show her,' I was thinking. 'I'll just go over there to Colorado and get work and send money back. I'll show her that I can take care of this family. She has no right to yell at me like that. She knows I love her and those kids more than anything on God's earth.'

"Hitching rides some, walking some, on and off a few trains, I got to Colorado three days later, along with several hundred other guys.

They sent us out to the camp and said be up at five to sign on for work. In the morning we got breakfast first then signed on for work crews. I signed for them to send my pay directly back home to your mother. I was going to call her that night after the job. She'd be happy to hear that I had some work.

"A bunch of us were on the truck going out to the site when a dynamite truck ran into us and blew up both trucks. We all died there on the spot. Just like that.

"My God! All I could think of was you two kids and your mother. Who would take care of you now? What could I do now?

"The next thing I knew, I was back at the house. I could see you were outside, and your mother and Sara were in the kitchen. Your mother was crying because I was missing then four days. She was scared something had happened to me and feeling sorry for what she said.

"I tried to get her to look at me. To hear me. But she acted like I wasn't there. Sara, too. I watched them go to the door. I heard the police sergeant tell her that it was best to face facts, your husband has walked out on you, ma'am. It happens all the time. He might come back. But he was thinking, 'The no-good bum. Imagine leaving a woman and two kids like that.'

"'No! That isn't what happened!' I was yelling right at them, but they couldn't hear me. 'Listen to me!' But she couldn't hear me.

"'Did you and your husband have a fight before he left? They typically leave after a fight, ma'am. Typically.'

"'No. No, sergeant, everything was fine, between him and me,' she lied.

"'Sorry, ma'am, there's nothing more we can do. Goodnight. You take care.'

"She said goodnight and shut the door. There was fury in her eyes.

"I tried, it seemed like forever, to get through to her, through to you and your sister. To tell you that I was dead. I didn't desert you. For God's sake, I didn't leave you. I went away to make some money for us. How could I ever leave you?

"Some others came about that time and took me to another place, someplace to rest where I couldn't keep trying to get your mother to listen to me. I was wearing myself out, and they got me settled down to rest for a long while. It seemed to me like no time at all, but it must have been, because here you are all grown up. Sara, too. I just heard that your mother was coming over there, so I was trying to find her, but they said to wait, she needs her rest. Don't worry, there will be plenty of time later. So, son, that's how I came to find you.

"I came here to tell you what really happened. It's clear that I should have come sooner, before you got to hating me so.

"Gabe. Listen, son. I did not leave you. I did not leave little Sara. I didn't run out on your mother. I was trying to do something to help the family. Just like she said I should. I was trying to do something. I had to do something!

"I was dead, Gabe. I never wanted to leave you, son!

"The project people, over at the dam, they were supposed to notify the families. But I don't know, God only knows why they never contacted your mother to tell her what harm came to me. Or to give her the benefit money she had coming. They had her name and address from when I signed on."

I'd heard enough, and I exploded. "Stop it, you bastard! God, how I hate you! Do you really expect me to believe your ghost story? Do you think I'm that big a fool? Why can't you just go away again and leave me alone!"

Then, damn him, when I looked again, I could see the dock right through his body. You bastard.

"I still don't know that what you're saying is true. Just because you're a goddamn ghost."

All my life I'd hated him so much. What was I supposed to do now? The hatred was part of every atom of my heart and soul. And I was supposed to just stop? Just stop just like that? Like, oh, Papa everything is okay now? All is forgiven, Papa, dear Papa?

"Son, look for the record. They keep the records. You'll find it. You can find out for yourself if it's true. You don't have to believe me if you don't want to."

Want to! I looked at him again, and he vanished before my eyes.

He was gone! I was alone on the dock. Just like that.

It took me over three months of hard work to find the accident records, but I did. Sure enough, there was his name, right there. I saw everything, just like he said. It felt like somebody had punched me in the stomach. Hard.

Some part of me was gone. A big part. I'd known myself all these years mostly by the hatred I had for him. I'd built my whole life on that hatred. Who was I now?

For over two years after that, I was in purgatory. I had to start over again. It was painful and frustrating and lonely. My daddy is dead. Papa didn't leave me, he died. He couldn't help it. He didn't want to go away. I had to grow myself up again from scratch.

My sister, Sara, didn't believe me and wouldn't even come with me to see the records.

"Leave me alone, Gabe! I don't care if it's true," she said. "I hate him, and I always will. Look what he did to Mama!"

It took a long time, but finally my heart started to open up again.

I saw him one more time, six years later. The night my daughter was born. Both of them were there at the hospital, my mother and my father. Together. Happy. Reunited. Smiling at me and my daughter.

I guess they wanted to see their first grandchild.

Chapter 13

Ancestral Eyes:
The Continuity of Family and Lineage

Our seed is lovingly planted in the fertile soil of lineage, and we spring forth into a family. A lineage is a larger pattern of souls who have come together for a common purpose. That we are born into a particular body, into a particular family at a particular time, is neither casual nor accidental. The pull of lineage and family embraces each of us from the moment of our conception, throughout our lives and into the hereafter. It is a vessel, another kind of body that we inhabit as surely as the physical body.

Our lineage is first spiritual. In order to express itself, the spirit takes on a genetic pattern, which is then expressed as a body, a mind, emotions, and spirit. It gives us the tools and the clay we need in order to create and know ourselves as souls. Our inheritance is passed along to us through the lifestream of the generations.

The connection with our ancestors transcends time and space. Those who came before us continue to be interested in us as individuals and as precious links in the ongoing chain of purposeful intention. We are all cells in a body. Family members nurture and care for the vessels of connection in this life and into the next. Ancestors embrace us throughout our lives and into the hereafter.

I hasten to add here that the power of your lineage has little to do with your feelings toward the people in your immediate family. Many of us, myself included, have felt at times that we were accidentally dropped off at the wrong house, maybe even the wrong planet. The power and presence of lineage does not concern just the superficial aspects of personality and relationship. The whole range of human relationships takes place within every family and every group, and just because you have a distant or even antagonistic relationship with your family, it doesn't mean you live outside the power and embrace of lineage.

Many people are blessed with the awareness of being a part of other spiritual bloodlines as well, such as an artistic, philosophic, or intellectual lineage. Strong bonds link us to those with whom we share values, interests, purpose, affinities, and states of being. These are families just as surely as are genetic relatives, and they may be our family of choice both here and in the hereafter.

It is common to hear of visitations from ancestors we knew when they were alive as well as from others who passed on before our birth. These fascinating stories suggest that lineage is of considerable concern to many in the hereafter, as seen in their desire to ensure continuity, impart wisdom, and offer us their guidance, healing, and confirmation. Ancestors may come to help you achieve something important that they themselves were unable to fulfill in their own lives here or to heal a wound that has been passed down through the generations. Long-held potential may come to fruition in you.

Our ancestors come to give assurance that they will be there to greet and celebrate our own passage into the afterlife as the great river of life flows eternally onward.

Gathering to celebrate the arrival of family

Celebration
by Suzanne Deats

I stayed with my aunt when I went back to the tiny West Texas town where both of my parents grew up. I went for my maternal grandmother's funeral. Auntie was my late father's sister and the only surviving member of that family.

Ninety-one at the time, Auntie was sweet and tough and a little ditzy. Although I asked her not to wait up for me that evening, when I tiptoed in the front door she was lying on the couch awake, fully dressed and ready to be sociable. She bobbed up like a little buoy, stuck her hearing aid in her ear, and commenced to tell me everything she had on her mind. I still remember her exact words.

"Suzanne, sit down. I want to tell you about the night your other grandmother, Granny Bertie, died. There was a real nice party with beautiful flowers everywhere. Of course, Bertie herself was right there, and I said to her, 'Oh, Bertie,' I said, 'I'm so glad you could be here at your own funeral party, and I'm happy Mother and Sister are here with us to celebrate, too.'"

Now, of course, Mother and Sister were long dead, but at Bertie's funeral they were all together, celebrating the new arrival.

Auntie was telling me that the veil between this life and the next is almost translucent and that toward the end, if one is paying attention, it is possible to move back and forth with very little effort. The fact that she perceived the passage as a celebration told me that she, too, would have a very easy time with it, and in fact that is just what happened.

Auntie herself soon joined her family, the generations who'd gone on before, who were certainly right there to greet her and celebrate her homecoming.

The continuity of souls

Mothers and Daughters

by Louisa Branscomb

My grandmother was the true matriarch in our family. She knew all the rules about how to be a genteel Southern woman. But don't let it fool you, she was tough as nails. She kept up the house, raised the children, and handled all the friendships and social responsibilities as well as maintained a spectacular yard and large garden.

It was the side of Grandmother that you didn't see that gave me my strong connection to her. She always said exactly what she thought, and this made me feel safe, because I didn't have to worry about something coming back to haunt me later. My grandmother had strong opinions about everything she bothered to have an opinion about at all.

When it came time for me to have a child, the person I first wanted to tell was my grandmother. I needed her blessing, and because I am in a same-sex relationship, I knew this could be controversial. To bless the birth of a child by alternative means, who will be raised by two women, was a lot to ask of a bedridden, ninety-three-year-old woman. Yet Grandmother had implicitly acknowledged my partner by accepting if not approving of her.

When the time came to tell Grandmother, my partner and I went into her room, and I sat down beside her on her bed. "Grandmother," I said, "I have decided I want to be a mother, and we are planning to have a child." Now, understand that I had much more prepared to say in my defense—all about how I had reached a good place in my career, how I felt I could provide for a child, all the "right" things.

But I didn't have a chance. "Oh, that's wonderful, Louisa!" Grandmother exclaimed without a second's hesitation. "How are you going to have it—by that, what do you call it, artificial insemination?" My grandmother was on top of things.

I did become pregnant, and in the interim my grandmother passed away.

To our deep sorrow, I lost the baby after three months.

When, two months later, Paula and I received a call from a physician asking if we were interested in adopting a child from a mother who has just become pregnant and could not care for the baby, I was thrown into tremendous conflict. It felt too soon to shift from grieving to celebrating. And I had lots of preconceived ideas about wanting my own biological child.

One night I was lying in bed struggling with whether to say yes to the adoption when suddenly my grandmother appeared at the foot of the bed. Somewhat like an opaque cloud, she was suspended in the center of the room. I hesitate to say it was the way angels look in Renaissance paintings, but that is how she looked.

Her presence was overwhelmingly strong, and she floated or hovered there just slightly above me. I heard her in my mind—maybe not her exact words, but her voice—very clearly, just as though she were speaking to me aloud.

Grandmother gave me words of deep comfort, telling me that it is okay for me to be a mother, it is okay for me to say yes to this unborn child. It is okay to celebrate our lives together as a family. It is okay to be happy.

Because of my grandmother's confirmation and blessing, we did adopt our daughter Olivia. She is now a thriving six-year-old, someone more like me in appearance and personality than I can imagine my own biological child could possibly be.

These experiences with my grandmother, my unborn child, and Olivia have made me feel a sense of place and significance in the ongoing cycle of life and of the life of the spirit. They have made real to me the succession of mothers and daughters, the continuity of souls.

Bringing peace, the river of life flows on

Grandfather's Voice

by Klaus Lumma

It is now about twenty-five years ago that the Old Green River flowing between the here and now and the afterworld allowed me to hear the most familiar voice of Opa.

On the train from Eschweiler to Aachen, I had an extraordinary experience. One morning, feeling very alone and sad, I realized that Opa, my grandfather, was now no more with me. Until his death we were very close; he was my personal counselor, guiding me, advising me with his wisdom and love. As my tears for Opa dropped onto my overcoat, I let them flow. When I could not see through my tears, I found that, instead of eyesight, I had a suddenly developing "earsight."

Through the watery tears, suddenly I could hear my Opa speaking. "Here I am with you," he said. "Trust in God. I am sitting next to God now. Trust in me, and if you ever again need advice, feel free to call for me. I will always be there for you, as I have always been." His presence flowed into me as I flowed into his voice.

Since this experience I have also known the presence of others— my ancestors, my mother, my father, and even our unborn daughter.

The voices of those ancestors now in the afterworld are the peace bringers of my life. They are a river that keeps flowing. It is my river of life.

Here is my belief: I believe in love that lasts longer than a person's lifetime, that love is the place where we human beings meet with God and where we encounter those who are already sitting next to God's armchair. And this love, I believe, is the only source of the advice and guidance we need for our daily lives.

The unbroken gaze of love

The Doll

by Mildred Larsen

It happened when I was a little girl, about seven. I was playing in my room that day because it was raining outside. I remember feeling that somebody was in the room with me. When I looked up I saw a woman, clear as day, sitting on my bed. I wasn't afraid at all because she seemed very kind and I could feel somehow that she loved me. She had a beautiful smile. The whole room glowed a kind of golden color.

The lady pointed to my favorite doll sitting up on the dresser, saying that it had been her doll when she was a little girl, given to her by her own mother. She said that my mother had never liked it much and that she was glad I did, and she said that the doll was named Elsie. I told her that I called her Elizabeth. The lady said that she was always with me, protecting me and loving me. I could feel these things as she spoke. She stayed for a few minutes and then gently said good-bye and faded away.

I was so excited that I raced downstairs and told my mother everything that had happened. As I spoke I saw tears come into her eyes. She cried quietly for a minute and then told me that the lady in my room was my grandmother, her mother, who had died when I was about two months old.

My mother was very different after that. Before that she was nervous and irritable sometimes. After that day she was calmer and had a peace about her that lasted all her life.

It made a big difference in my life, too. I have always felt protected and watched over by the loving presence of my family who came before me, and I have felt myself as part of an ongoing life that will continue after I'm gone. And I have never been afraid of death.

The fabric of family is woven across time and space

The Inheritance

by Georgeanne Paul

While I was in the middle of washing the dinner dishes in a sink full of soapy water, the strangest feeling came over me. My father was calling for me, and I could feel his presence as if he were right there in the room with me, saying my name.

So there at my home in Montana, I sat down in meditation to attune with him where he was living in Colorado. We had been estranged most of my adult life because Dad had disapproved of my living with a boyfriend many years before, and somehow we had never been able to repair the damage, remaining distant and wounded. I had accepted the idea that we might not ever be reconciled.

As I got quiet, something extraordinary happened. I felt Dad with me. Then all at once, I could feel the presence of all of his family members who had already died, some many, many years before. Brother, sister, parents, all now deceased, were there. Suddenly a stream, then a river, of ancestors came pouring in and through me.

The flow of ancestral presence and energy was indecipherable to the rational mind, but I knew with certainty that I was receiving generations of wisdom, knowledge that my family and my lineage wanted me to carry in my bones and blood for the rest of my life and to pass on to my children and on to their children. Stunned by the magnitude of this experience and its gifts, I suddenly realized that I was receiving my inheritance! Not only that, I was receiving a balm, a salve to heal the family wounds between me and my father. Such a healing balm enables the generations to stay connected across lifetimes.

From that time on, a veil lifted between me and my dad. I went to visit him just a week later, knowing it would be the last time I would see him on this earth. Close for the first time in decades, we had an easy and happy time together. All of the pain and bitterness were gone, and once again love flowed between us.

Before he had surgery in September, I was able to tell Dad that I was sorry that we had not been closer and to let him know about the deep regret that had been so long with me—how much I regretted that we had wasted all those precious years, bitter and estranged from each other.

"We are close now," he said, "so what difference does it make?"

That was our last conversation. My dad did not recover. Yet I was at peace, having a deeper connection now not only to him but also to his family. The knowledge that I carry their wisdom and their love in the very fabric of my being changes me and how I live in the world.

A gift from those who came before, passed on and multiplied

The Lady in Lace

by Catherine Ann Cobeaga

With a faltering marriage and intermittent health problems, I was feeling emotionally drained and spiritually abandoned. My quest for healing and wholeness in body, mind, and spirit seemed, ironically, to be tearing my life apart.

Becoming weaker and weaker over a period of months, I had to pry myself out of bed to take care of my family and home. As one diagnostic test after another showed that everything was normal, I certainly began to question the meaning of that word!

One Sunday afternoon as I lay on the bed, exhausted and sick, hot tears filled my eyes. Feeling totally alone, it seemed that I was completely unable to change anything in my life. As I drifted into a half-dream state, I prayed for courage, for the strength to endure with my sanity intact until some answers came. Some of the emotional pain subsided, and I found myself drifting, floating on a cloud over a beautiful field of wildflowers. It was lovely, and in that moment I felt safe and peaceful.

I suddenly realized I was on the ground, sitting among the flowers, watching a woman in white approaching from a great distance. I was filled with anticipation and curiosity as the woman moved toward me quickly and effortlessly and then stopped about five or six feet from where I sat. She wore the most beautiful long, white, high-collared lace dress, and her long hair was pulled back softly from her face.

I looked deeply into her eyes. Somehow I knew her, but from where? She smiled with such depth of love and tenderness that my heart swelled within me, and I wept, feeling the tears soak my face.

"Who are you?" I asked. Her answer unfolded in my awareness without a single word being spoken. She was my grandmother!

The beautiful woman before me was my mother's mother, who had died in an influenza epidemic when Mother was barely six months old. She smiled again when I asked her why she had come to me. Speaking directly to my heart and soul, my grandmother explained to me that I was going through a uniquely feminine experience, something that is part of the emotional and spiritual lives of all women, the phase of a woman's life that often brings great pain and suffering.

She said that my own healing of this passage would bring healing to the other women of my earthly family. I knew then that as I endured the process and eventually healed myself, my daughter and her daughter and all the women in the future would be able to move through this time with much greater ease.

Grandmother wanted me to know that I was not alone and that, just as she had watched over my mother, she had always been with me and would always be watching over me. I learned from my grandmother that day that I came from a lineage of women of spiritual strength and presence. Understanding that I had within myself the strength and ability to endure and bring healing to my present experience, I knew that I would grow from it and be able to help the women who would come after me. This passage, successfully navigated, would greatly enhance my own spiritual and emotional journey toward wholeness as well as that of succeeding generations.

Returning to full consciousness a minute later, I felt as though I had slept in Grandmother's healing embrace. Tears of gratitude and awe flowed through me.

The following year, when visiting my parents, I asked about my grandmother. My mother got out the one surviving photograph of her mother. It shows my grandmother at her wedding, radiant in her long, white, high-collared, lace dress, her long hair pulled back softly from her smiling face.

Chapter 14

Emissaries of Love:
Symbolic Messengers

A special kind of visitation is one in which you are visited by an emissary rather than by the person who has died. The emissary clearly and unmistakably is the carrier of a message for you from the other world. Embodying the spirit of your loved one for that moment, this messenger has been sent on a unique, always highly meaningful mission of a very special nature—to reveal to you that life continues beyond the body and so does love.

So that you will make the connection, the emissary must be so personally meaningful or so out of the ordinary that you will recognize its importance. These bearers of greetings and good tidings from the afterlife may be people or animals, animate or inanimate objects, or specific occurrences and happenings. The very personal symbolic content, coupled with its timing and location, cause us to pay attention and thus realize that we are in the midst of magic. The visitation creates a force field of numinous energy, which holds us in its enchantment as our hearts open to receive loving greetings from the afterlife.

The synchronicity of the highly charged appearance, its presence in a very particular time and place and in a very particular way, tells you that it is not mere coincidence or chance, not wishful thinking.

It is an intentional affirmation of the very particularized bond of love that exists between you and your loved one. In this moment you are given a sign that is as clearly a message as is a pile of carefully arranged stones left to mark your path through the woods. As you turn your attention toward the emissary, you hear a symbolic, nonverbal message meant just for you: "Be comforted, I am here, I am with you."

Wonderful stories of emissary visitations abound: mysterious appearances of special flowers or books or feathers or butterflies in unlikely places or the strange dance of a heart-shaped balloon or the insistent song of a bird on a special occasion. It can be the appearance of certain people or animals, even unusual events. It can be anything, as long as it is something specific, speaking to you in the special vocabulary of intimacy that you and your loved one share.

The enchantment comes in the meaningfulness of the appearance coupled with its timing and location. It must be highly symbolic and meaningful so that you will not only notice it but also perceive its intention. For example, if neither of you had any special relationship to roses, you might not recognize a sign that appears in roses. But if your mother loved roses and one appears on your pillow on her birthday, that is meaningful and quite different from seeing roses every day in the window of the florist's shop.

The variety of symbolic visitations is endless. In each case something profoundly relevant to the person who has died, something rich in shared meaning, comes to our attention as the carrier of a special message. The emissary, whatever its form, is a presence announcing connection.

Recognition may dawn because of an energy shift, as in the story of an unexpected meeting with a raven. Not only did the unusual circumstances surrounding his appearance suggest that this was no ordinary bird and no ordinary moment, but also the atmosphere itself was charged with a heightened energy, leaving no doubt that this was an extraordinary event. A shimmering energy field proclaimed the sacred territory.

Those who carry the messages, the emissaries themselves, are they real? Are they spirit? Are there beings who mediate between the worlds? I feel that it is irrelevant whether the emissary is a material part of this world who is momentarily acting as a representative or an ethereal materialization emerging from the invisible. It is possible that both kinds of emissaries exist. I can imagine that a deer might take on the role for few minutes and then return to foraging in the woods. A child might unknowingly be the carrier of a symbolic gesture as she brings greetings in a certain way at a special time. She is a living, material creature who is allowing herself, knowingly or not, to be the bearer of tidings from the other side. And, I imagine, too, that it sometimes happens that some bearer of grace arises out of the unseen, manifests momentarily to deliver a message, only to disappear back into the invisible when its work is done. Who can tell of these things?

Through an immediate recognition, a knowing, we experience the emissary as the bearer of a loving, healing message of comfort and hope. It is clear that we are being touched by a great mystery from another realm as the emissary bridges the apparent distance between two worlds. The visitation opens us to the vast mystery of life, and for a moment we touch its magic.

Always one to move in mysterious ways

The Work of a Special Agent
by Maura Conlon-McIvor

In the fall and winter of 1992, I spent several months, along with my husband, working at a hospital in the West Indies. The hospital was staffed by an international crew of volunteer medical and support personnel. We were on the island of St. Lucia, surrounded by lush banana fields, towering pitons, and vibrant people.

While living on St. Lucia, I commemorated, on December 5, the one-year anniversary of my father's death. My father, Joseph Conlon, was the quintessential tough man, a lawyer and FBI agent for twenty-seven years. From him I learned how to be masculine in the world, to be career minded, logical, rational, analytical. Indeed, as a kid, I wanted to become an FBI agent myself.

However, from my father I also learned the limitations of this masculine countenance, knowing that for each ounce of his distant reserve there existed an equivalent longing for expression, connection, and a sense of belonging. I was witness to this paradox thanks to my youngest brother, Joseph, Jr., who was born in 1966 with Down's syndrome. My father worked for years to improve the lives of people like my brother, holding celebrity fund-raising dinners throughout Los Angeles to build private, spiritually based group homes. My father was obsessed, not only by the FBI's ten most wanted, but also by those we call mentally retarded. Their innocence, vulnerability, and love captured him as if by net, as if by trance, never letting him go.

These thoughts I shared with my friend, Belle, another hospital volunteer, as we sat in a small village church in St. Lucia on that hot, sticky Sunday. I told her stories about my father's love for the mentally retarded as we waited for the December 5 mass to begin, which I had arranged earlier in the week to be celebrated in his honor.

Leaning over to Belle, I whispered, "Even on my wedding day, as he walked me up the aisle, my father spotted a Down's syndrome girl sitting at the edge of the church pew. He stopped suddenly, left my side, walked over, and kissed her on the cheek. I was shocked. Embarrassed. But you should have seen the beaming face of that little girl."

Just as I finished this sentence, the doors of the village church in St. Lucia swung open. A Down's syndrome man wearing a brown suit and tie entered. He walked slowly up the aisle. He genuflected at the altar, turned right, and continued walking directly toward the pew where I sat. He came closer, looked at me straight in the eye, and sat down behind me. Tears shot straight down my cheeks, and my limbs trembled. I looked over to Belle and could see her in shock as well.

I knew my father was close by. The appearance of this fellow with Down's was not coincidental. I knew that, for whatever reason, my father was returning to me on the first anniversary of his death in the form of this gentle, Down's syndrome man. But why? Was there a message for me? I turned around and looked into the man's eyes. What was I to hear? The message was not forthcoming.

Though I shared this story with my family and close friends, I wondered, how could it be packaged into a nice, neat vernacular out of which I could make sense? The incident became a perplexing mystery, a beguiling memory. Still, my father was not about to leave me alone. Not yet.

One year later, again on December 5, I was commuting by train to Portland, Oregon, for my weekly film class. Sitting in a nearly empty train car, I reminisced to myself about this anniversary day the year before, when that Down's fellow appeared out of nowhere in St. Lucia. Just then, I began to hear clumsy footsteps approaching from behind on the train where I sat.

Soon enough, the shuffling couple arrived. I looked up to see a mentally retarded couple, one of them with Down's syndrome. They sat down next to me. "Hello," the man said to me, "my name is Richard, and this is my wife, Mary."

The year before when I was sitting in that St. Lucia village church, I cried when I realized that my father's spirit was visiting with me. This year I could only chuckle, saying, "Okay, Dad, what are you trying to tell me?"

I spoke in easy sentences with Richard and Mary until the train pulled into the station. Then I didn't want to let them out of my sight. Who were they? Why did they mysteriously appear this day, the anniversary of my father's death?

I remember the last words my father spoke to me before he passed away. They were about my brother: "Who will take care of Joe?" he asked. "Who will take care of Joe?"

I assured him Joe would always be all right.

The story continues, thanks in large part to the spirit of my relentless father, the man who was so much more than an FBI agent, who always worked in mysterious ways and best when he traveled undercover.

Joining in to celebrate a very special family occasion

The Honey Eater
by Marguerite Doig

Two days after his funeral in New Zealand, our beloved son, Matthew, stood beside us looking exactly as he had before his death except that he appeared to be a few years older and quite a bit taller. Beckoning to me and his father to follow him, Matthew walked with us down a path where we had often walked together when he was alive. Feeling no fear, we felt, instead, very calm and filled with peace. Though after a while Matthew indicated that he had to leave us, those precious moments with our son left both my husband and me with a deep comfort and feelings of peace.

Some years later we traveled to a very special family gathering for the baptism of our new grandchild. As we all sat together companionably talking, I became very aware of Matthew, and I knew with certainty that he was present. Just then someone remarked how very much they wished Matthew were with us. Exactly at that moment, a little bird appeared on the window ledge and began dancing and hopping about and pecking excitedly on the glass. It was a honey eater, which, though a very common bird in other parts of Australia, is *never* seen in that particular area.

Suddenly, all at once, everyone began laughing together. We all remembered that because of his great fondness for honey, we used to tease Matthew, calling him "our own honey eater!"

It was a wonderful gift from the Lord that we were blessed with these loving experiences of Matthew's presence to reassure us that he lives on and is always with us, especially on such special family occasions.

Dancing across the boundaries between this world and the next

Magda's Dance
by Murray Stein

I had known Magda for more than ten years, and in the course of our friendship we had had many profound conversations. She was Catholic and religious and believed without reservation in the reality of God and the afterlife. I am a Protestant rationalist and have a stubborn habit of conscious doubt. I was a skeptic about such matters, but I did not question the sincerity of her beliefs and never challenged her certainties. I would simply listen respectfully when we entered that territory.

Magda became crippled in later life and was confined to a wheelchair. She enjoyed telling me that when she died and went to heaven the first thing she wanted to do there was to dance. She loved to imagine her body whole again and capable of full movement. This is what she looked forward to most of all, even more than to meeting loved ones and the religiously famous. In her youth she had loved to dance, and she grieved the loss of her physical mobility and independence.

Shortly before Magda's death, I read in a newspaper that Pope John Paul II had confirmed the sainthood of Edith Stein and would canonize her in Rome at St. Peter's. Magda had connections in Rome, so I asked her if she thought it would be possible for me to obtain tickets for the canonization. She made a phone call and assured me that when the time came for Edith Stein's canonization I would have seats. I thanked her profusely.

After Magda received a diagnosis of terminal pancreatic cancer, she died quickly, choosing to ask her doctors to withhold unrealistic treatment. She was prepared to leave her body. On our last visit together, we kissed her farewell, wishing her a good journey into the valley of the shadow of death. I knew she was as well prepared for this final experience of life as anyone can be.

On the day of Magda's funeral we were surprised when we found that the time and place of her service had been changed. It would be held in a larger church several hours later in another part of town. Our car had been parked in a lovely garden behind the home, and as we drove away I said to my wife to check the backseat. Something had gotten into our car and was flapping around in the rear window. It was an extremely hot day in Chicago, and the windows and doors had been closed tight because the interior of the car was cooled by air conditioning.

My wife turned to the rear window and exclaimed in surprise, "It's a butterfly!"

"Impossible," I said. "How could a butterfly have gotten into our car, all locked up?"

But, sure enough, it was a large brown butterfly with bits of blue on its wings. And it was determined to stay in the rear window of our car for the whole trip. I opened all the windows, offering it an escape and hoping it would fly away, but it refused to leave. Even after the funeral service, the butterfly continued to accompany us as we drove homeward. We began to speak of it jokingly as Magda.

"Well, okay, Magda has decided to come home with us!"

When we got home it was dark. My wife reached her hand into the back of the car in hopes that the butterfly would now accept the invitation to make an exit. Previously this had not worked, but this time the butterfly hopped onto her hand and sat tight. We called our friend Joyce, also Magda's friend, from inside the house to come out and see Magda, too.

As we stood together outside under a streetlight, Magda the butterfly jumped to the ground and began doing an amazing dance at our feet. Round and round she went in a frenzy of motion. Suddenly I remembered Magda's ardent hope to dance again in eternity, and I burst out, "Well, Magda, I see you've made it! You're dancing!"

At this moment I was no longer a Protestant rationalist, and my agnosticism had vanished completely. The boundaries between this world and the next were breached. I could only believe that in this moment we saw our friend Magda in the form of a butterfly. The butterfly flew off, and we knew we had witnessed something extraordinary.

The next morning our friend Joyce telephoned. She said, "Do you know what happened to the butterfly? It came home with me in my

car! And then it flew off in the direction of Dorothy's garden."
Dorothy had been one of Magda's best lifelong friends.

About a year passed, and, thanks to Magda's earlier intervention,
I was able to get tickets for Edith Stein's canonization in Rome in St.
Peter's Square on October 11, 1998. I had been interested in the
case of Edith Stein for some years. She was a Jewish convert to
Roman Catholicism who became a Carmelite nun in the 1930s and
died a Jewish-Christian martyr in Auschwitz in 1942. She was also a
distinguished philosopher and had been the favorite pupil of the
philosopher Edmund Husserl.

I was in a state of heightened anticipation as my wife and I and a
couple of Roman friends made our way to the choice seats reserved
for us, thanks to the help of Magda and her friends in Rome.

The service itself was deeply moving, of course. This aged pope, so
humbled by physical decline, who could barely move forward out of
St. Peter's to his chair on the platform under his own power, presided
for three hours over a service that was very special for him, too.

Both he and Edith Stein were born and grew up in Poland, and
he has been intensely involved in healing the historical conflict
between Christians and Jews. The ritual, the music, the crowd of
seventy thousand people from all parts of the world, the illustrious
cardinals and politicians on the platform with the pope—Helmut
Kohl was there—all contributed to the impressive effect. The invisible world became quite palpable in that atmosphere, understandably so.

But nothing could have prepared me for what happened as the
service was drawing to a close.

As we were standing for the final prayer of benediction, the pope
began intoning his blessing in Latin. The text of this prayer is presented in four languages, and I was following the pope's unclear
diction as best I could. When he arrived at the line *Ex hoc nunc et
usque in saeculum, Von nun an bis in Ewigkeit, Ora e sempre, Now
and forever,* an astonishing thing happened. A brown butterfly with
bits of blue color on its wings appeared out of nowhere from that
crowd of thousands and alighted on the open page before me. It
perched quietly on the words *Ora e sempre* and stayed there.

At first I could not take in what was happening. I had seen no butterflies in that sea of human faces before this moment. I was stunned. Where had this butterfly come from? We were in the middle of a huge crowd in a giant city, not in a garden. I looked around in astonishment and could hardly believe my eyes. There were no other butterflies to be seen.

My wife gasped, too. "It's the same butterfly!" she whispered. Sure enough, it appeared identical to the butterfly in Chicago. (Our friends beside us did not know the previous story of Magda the butterfly, but they were also surprised to see a butterfly in this unlikely place and sitting on my prayer book.)

Is this Magda? I wondered to myself in amazement.

The butterfly took to the air as the pope said "Amen" and disappeared in the direction of the altar some one hundred meters in front of us. My fantasy is that it joined the other spirits and angels so palpably present in Piazza San Pietro that bright day in October.

Like a love message in a bottle

My Sweet Valentine
by Medora Nankervis

It was Valentine's Day when a dear friend came to visit, bringing a heart-shaped, helium-filled balloon. It was silver on one side and had "I love you" written all over the other side. I hung it next to the red balloon that I'd brought home earlier that morning.

Only two days later my dearest friend, my beloved husband, Mel, died of cancer in the hospital bed we'd set up in the living room of our country house, which he'd hand-built from our forest trees. The bed was next to a big window where he could watch the great outdoors. So that he could enjoy the festive balloons, I put the two of them, one red and one silver, in front of the windows.

Mel, a Paul Bunyan of a man, was seemingly indestructible until cancer came, conquering his body though never his spirit. We were blessed with time to declare and reaffirm our love in the home he built and loved. We had time to say our good-byes. "I'll be there waiting for you, with bells on," he promised, "when it's time for you to come, too." We clung together and cried.

Scattering Mel's ashes in the forest he loved, we celebrated his life, his brilliant mind and gifts. This was a man who could do anything he set his mind on. He could move a mountain as easily as blowing on a balloon.

The pain of missing my beloved stayed with me. It is physical, you know, rather like an endless kick in the stomach, a constriction of the heart. It affects breathing and powers of concentration, as a sob or tears unexpectedly pop up. Not wanting to let go of him, I'd cry out, "Where did you go? What do you see? Do you think of me?"

After a time I was alone, and the realities of everyday living returned. My dreaded job annually was the federal and state income taxes. I put it off, feeling much too muddled by grief to think of numbers. Now, with time running out, I got up one morning at 4 A.M. to avoid interruption and went to work at my desk.

Two hours later, pushing my chair back and stretching my arms into the air, I suddenly caught a movement in the corner of my eye near the loft skylight, where first light was beginning to appear. Turning toward it, I saw what caught my eye. It was the silver heart-shaped balloon I'd let go of days before, inching its way across the loft from the skylight. Sinking down and then rising up again, it crawled over the railing and rose just as slowly over to the cathedral ceiling. Finding a path between beams, the balloon slanted downward to cross the large room and go directly to the red Valentine balloon on the other side.

I had to leave the desk in order to follow the movement. Barely breathing, I saw the silver heart-shaped balloon move at a snail's pace across the living room to the window beside the red one. Then it stopped, its silver side facing me. Ever so slowly, it inched back just enough to give itself room to turn 180 degrees. Then it displayed its other side to me, the side with the writing all over it. "I love you! I love you! I love you!" it said to me! And then the balloon did a little a bow, a dip, as though it were a hat.

Enchanted and amazed, I felt Mel's love coming into me by way of the balloon, and in that moment I remembered a card he'd given me months before. On it he'd recorded his voice so that every time I'd open the card, I'd hear him saying, "I love you! I love you! I love you! Your sweetheart, Mel."

My grief-ridden mind, body, and spirit began to heal.

Life is unimaginably more vast and magical than we know

The Raven

by Lee Lawson

A strange insistent sound, almost like a metallic duck quacking, broke the immense silence of early morning. Our home sits atop a canyon overlooking thousands of acres of rugged coastal mountains near the Pacific Ocean at the southern tip of the Big Sur Coast.

"What is that sound? Do you hear it?" I called out to Martin from my studio.

"Yes," my husband called back. "It's a bird, and I think you should come take a look!"

I joined him in the garden, and Martin said a huge black bird had just tried to perch on his shoulder three times. As he spoke, the bird suddenly reappeared and landed on the ground directly in front of us.

Astonished, we gazed at a large, blue-black, one-eyed wild raven.

From that moment on, for the next three days, the raven stayed with us every minute of each day. From the first he was in constant physical contact with us, insisting on touching us whenever he could, pecking or nuzzling very gently at fingers, clothes, arms, legs, shoulders. Whatever he could touch, he touched. In constant eye contact with one or the other of us, he followed us everywhere, mostly walking on the ground, not flying. When Martin walked about fifty yards out to the well, Raven walked along next to him, just like a dog trotting along by his side. In fact, like a particular dog had done until just the night before Raven appeared.

Our most beloved dog, Lily, had died that night. Lily was a huge beautiful, snow white German shepherd with coal black eyes and nose who could suddenly look like a variety of different animals— most often a polar bear, sometimes a deer or a unicorn. Children mistook her for a white pony.

Lily had become ill in December and had weakened rapidly until at last, ten days later, she died, leaving us utterly grief-stricken. It felt like my heart dropped right out of my body.

Lily and I'd had an extraordinary relationship, a bond that transcended time, space, species. For three years before Lily's birth, several times a week, I dreamed with this extraordinary being, who appeared in the dream form of a huge, beautiful, white dog. In my dreams and later, after her birth, she was friend, teacher, spirit, angel, guide, parent, child. A bond that was ancient and sacred existed between us.

Every day for ten years of her life our time together was magical. Lily and I were together every day and night for those ten years. She lay under my easel as I painted, slept by the bed until morning, and then jumped into bed when Martin vacated it for work. Lily went where I went. We were together twenty-four hours a day.

Then, after ten years, Lily was gone. Martin and I were thrust into immense grief as we went to bed the night of her death, just after Christmas. Waking up early the next morning feeling the full force our loss, I went to the studio and Martin went out into the yard, each to grieve in silence.

It was then that the huge, blue-black, one-eyed raven who sounded like a metallic duck landed at our feet.

From that moment on we were swept up into another dimension, transported into another realm. It was an overlay upon this world, one more electrical, more dimensional, more magical. We were in a force field in Raven's presence. All day as the raven went about with us, we felt the palpable presence and electricity of enchantment. It's not that we lived in ordinary space while a bird tagged along. We shifted into a state similar to lucid dreaming. Very much wide awake, we felt every sense heightened to perceive another dimension of life.

It was immediately apparent that the raven was a visitation from Lily. The raven wasn't Lily, but it was clearly and certainly from Lily;

it had come to us because of Lily, maybe even with her. We realized even as it was happening that it was impossible to understand what we were experiencing.

The very ineffability of the experience demanded an extraordinary degree of presence from us. Since we didn't know how long the raven would be with us, we had to assume that any minute, any second, he could fly away and not come back. We had to open fully every second to the gift of his presence, and we both felt hyperaware and awake during this amazing visit.

For three days Raven followed us everywhere, acting very little like a bird and very much like a dog. Walking like Lily, tilting his head like Lily, sitting, looking, radiating love—all with the same mannerisms and gestures as Lily's but in the shape of a raven.

Never more than a foot or two from one of us, Raven was usually much closer, always looking right into our eyes, focused completely on our faces. Just like Lily, he wanted to play, and many times he brought Lily's toys in from the yard. He picked up Lily's favorite sticks in his mouth and tossed them around in front of our feet.

On the afternoon of the third day it suddenly occurred to me that I should take pictures. I snapped several shots—Raven and Martin together, Raven landing and sitting on Martin's head, gazing soulfully into his eyes, nibbling on his shirt. Every minute of Raven's visit was charged with magic, and we opened ourselves as fully as possible to receive it. He made us so aware, minute by minute, that nothing in the material world is permanent, that life is a constant experience of beholding and letting go, releasing life into the next moment. The only certainty is that the next moment will bring change.

We did not know, as we went to sleep on the third night, that the raven would not come back the next day. He has never returned.

Though Martin and I grieve deeply for Lily, we continue to receive the grace of those extraordinary ten years plus three days. A sense of the preciousness of each moment and each day stays with us. There is no knowing what life holds, and to receive the blessing and gift of life you must stand in the present with an open heart. Throughout Raven's visit I had the overwhelming sensation that life is immeasurably more vast and magical than we could possibly imagine.

Three postscripts follow this story.

P.S. 1: During the following two days, several animals unexpectedly visited our house. A large frog hopped through the living room, a strange cat was found sitting on the kitchen counter, two lizards came inside, a strange dog ran through the house and out the back door, and two hummingbirds were in the house when no doors or windows had been open for their entry. Most unusual of all, I heard someone at the front door, and when I opened it, there on the step sat a large white pig!

P.S. 2: I wrote to my friend Paula telling her about the raven visitation. Paula told me that when she got my letter, she and her husband Donald were standing at their kitchen window reading it and looking at the photographs when a large black raven suddenly landed right before their eyes, just a few feet away, directly outside the kitchen window.

P.S. 3: As I sat writing this account, just moments ago, I heard a strange sound and got up to investigate. I was astonished by the synchronicity when I saw that a bird had flown into the house and down the long hallway. It was perching above the doorway to my studio, just a few feet away from where I now sit writing. After a while I climbed up on a chair and, cupping the bird in my hands, carried her outside. When I opened my hands to free her, she sat calmly in my palms for about five minutes before she finally flew away. I could feel her gentle heartbeat like a tiny drum against my skin as I looked at her beautiful bird's body up close.

Eternity looks at us through the eyes of love

Heart to Heart
by Sue Derozier

My dog Shane was an extraordinary and loving companion who saw me through some very difficult times. When we moved to an extremely isolated, remote area in upper Wisconsin, he chose a favorite spot out on the north shore of Lake Superior, and we went there together again and again. It was a place where he could run free, and he and I spent many of our happiest hours there.

Shane was my happiness during a time when there was no other joy in my life. The sight of him running to greet me with such pure joy in his eyes and excitement for life always renewed me in spirit and filled my heart at a time when very little else did.

My loss, pain, and grief were tremendous when, while I was visiting my family in upper Michigan, Shane was killed by a car.

One day after he died I drove to the north shore of the lake, far away from anything, out to our old favorite place. As I sat alone sunning myself, suddenly I looked up to see a wild fawn standing in the path right near me. I don't know how to say this except to say that I knew without any doubt in my heart it was Shane.

In the moment of recognition, the fawn cocked its head and looked directly at me, exactly the way Shane had looked at me so many times. I clearly, unmistakably saw Shane gazing at me through those eyes. I don't know how long the fawn and I stayed there in stillness, silently looking into each other's eyes, communing heart to heart. Finally he began moving down the hill and toward the road. Because of what had happened to Shane the dog, I immediately became alarmed, worried that the fawn, too, would be hit by a car and killed.

As these thoughts crossed through my mind, the fawn stopped and looked back at me, knowingly, acknowledging my concern. He then went forward, slowly approached the road, and carefully looked both ways before crossing. Once safely on the other side, he gave me one long last look and disappeared into the woods.

I can't tell you how wonderful it was for me to have those precious healing moments. They reminded me, as I had been reminded so many times before, that you cannot lose the ones you love. Life and love are eternal, and I know that as long as love remains, I am not alone.

In Closing

Oneness

The moment I die,
  I will try to come back to you.
  as quickly as possible.
I promise that it will not take long.

Isn't it true
  I am already with you,
    as I die in each moment?
 I come back to you
    in every moment.
Just look, feel my presence.

If you want to cry,
  please cry.
And know
  that I will cry with you.
The tears you shed

will heal us both.
Your tears are mine.

The earth I tread this morning
  transcends history.
Spring and Winter are both present in this moment,
  The young leaf and the dead leaf are really one.

My feet touch deathlessness
  and my feet are yours.
Walk with me now.
  Let us enter the dimension of oneness
  And see the cherry tree blossom in Winter.

Why should we talk about death?
  I do not need to die
    To be back with you.

THICH NHAT HANH

Many blessings are inherently a part of every visitation. The wonderful visitation stories you have read hint at the mystery and magic to be encountered in the theater of eternity. This life on earth is one stage of many upon which we experience ourselves and the sacred. Visitations point to the possibility of a larger, multidimensional stage, as well as other stages, other stories, other times and places, and other souls with whom we gather for the dance of life. When this dance is over we move on, to dance again.

Our loved ones who have passed on are always with us; there is no other place to go. Everything is here, and every time is now. They share our tears, our joys, and our lives because they have not left us, only become, for a while, invisible to our eyes.

As Thich Nhat Hanh's beautiful poem suggests, Spring and Winter are both present in this moment because everything is present in this moment. There is no other moment. Eternity knows no time. On this earthly stage we use time as a vessel that gives form and shape to our expression and experience.

In writing this book and collecting stories from hundreds of people, I have given much thought to visitations and how my own life has been influenced by these extraordinary experiences. I have been affected by them on many levels and in ways that I do not yet begin to understand. Visitations have helped me through the difficult periods of great mourning that I myself have experienced, having lost, beginning early in life, several members of my immediate and extended family and a number of close friends.

A visitation gives me a promise that even though the suffering now is very real and sometimes devastating, a time of reunion will come. The fabric of my life, rent when my loved one passes out of my sight, will once again be made whole. A visitation gives me the knowledge that even though I understand little about why and how life goes on, it does go on for all of us. Existence is a safe place for me and the people I love. I cannot lose my life, and I cannot lose other souls who are dear to me. Our survival is assured.

The blessing and healing are given to all, not just to those who have personally experienced the return of a loved one. All of us may receive healing as we read stories of the ongoing care that comes to bless, comfort, and reassure. Like a pebble dropped in a pond, the sharing of these precious moments allows the blessing of the visitation to ripple out, touching us all with their grace and message of comfort.

Every reunion is brought about in the service of love, and its deepest message is that as life continues, our loved ones continue to care for our well-being. They are always with us in spirit and care about the events of our lives. Retaining their individuality, our loved ones in the hereafter still have their unique characteristics, opinions, and personal perspectives, albeit from a larger vantage point.

Because of their new perspective, and knowing something of the greater soul purposes, they help us with guidance and direction in our spiritual lives. Giving clear indications of concern for our emotional and psychological states, our loved ones demonstrate that they still care deeply for our feelings, for our sufferings and confusions as well as our joys and realizations. Every story tells us that our lives are seen as precious and important and that our choices and experiences, large and small, are meaningful for our own growth as well as for the life of the larger whole. We are all cells in the body of life, and each of us is of ultimate importance to the health and harmony of life's body.

Whether they are soothing our grief, sharing our joy and suffering, saying good-bye, revealing to us the splendors of the afterlife, expressing concerns with our daily lives here and now, guarding and protecting us, or healing us and helping us to find peace of mind, our loved ones assure us that we are never alone. Even when we cannot feel or sense their presence in our lives, we can know that we are ever connected to the larger family of creation by that most intimate and far-reaching bond, the heart. Love transcends time and space and allows us to live in the dimension of oneness where together we can see the cherry tree bloom in winter.

Beauty, enchantment, and, above all, mystery characterize each visitation from the afterlife. This mysterious grace comes as it will, not as we will. A visitation may come to someone who is not in any way consciously receptive to mystical states while not to someone else who is utterly receptive and open and greatly desiring of a meeting. We wonder why a mother comes to one child and not to the others or why one life is saved by a loving presence when others are not so protected.

Questions such as these cannot be answered in any earthly terms. Each of us must go within and find our own way to be at peace with these mysteries. For many, these experiences create as many questions as answers—existential, spiritual questions about the nature of this life we live. Such questions demand that we deepen our communion with every aspect of ourselves, not in order to find specific answers but rather to enlarge and temper the vessel that we are. Then, able to encompass greater and greater awareness, we expand our capacity for deeper, more meaningful experiences of knowing ourselves as multidimensional beings alive in a spiritual universe.

The stories, like the visitation experiences themselves, are doorways, passageways into another understanding of reality. If you allow them to flow in without judgments, they will feed and enliven and heal you where you need it the most. For some, the stories may be symbolic food, providing metaphors that awaken and enrich the soul. Others will experience the stories as validation of long-held beliefs about survival after death and the continuity of life. For still others, the stories will feed the "don't know" part of their souls and increase their capacity to embrace ever deeper and greater aspects of being.

I am occasionally asked how I know that visitations are a good thing, not the work of "dark forces." My only response is this: "By their fruits you shall know them." My own experience, and that of those who have shared their experiences with me, is overwhelmingly that visitations are a blessing. They are a catalyst for healing and wholeness, for turning toward, not away from, spiritual awareness, and for instilling in us a deeper reverence for the sacred gift of life.

An Invitation
to Send Your Story

If you have had a visitation from a beloved person or animal and would like to share your story, please type it, double-spaced, in up to 1,500 words. Include your name, address, phone, fax, and e-mail address. Your story will be considered for inclusion in a subsequent volume of *Visitations from the Afterlife*.

You may send correspondence and visitation stories to:

Lee Lawson
630 Quintana Rd., #326
Morro Bay, CA 93442
USA

Stories may also be sent by e-mail to: lee@leelawson.com

For more about *Visitations from the Afterlife* or for information about Lee Lawson's paintings and art reproductions, please visit the Web site at:

www.leelawson.com

Acknowledgments

Jeanne Achterberg is both midwife and godmother to *Visitations from the Afterlife.* It was she whom I first told about Harry's "gift," and it was she who, without hesitation, encouraged me to accept the gift and believe that I could birth it into the world.

I am ever grateful to my beloved friend and soul sister, Clarissa Pinkola Estés, for her enormous heart, contagious laughter, passion for creativity, and for her love. Her foreword to this book is an extraordinary gift of heart and healing, a reminder to celebrate "God's business" by opening ourselves to the mystery and magic of our lives. Clarissa is a force of enchantment.

My gratitude to Stephanie Laidman Tade, my literary agent, who listened to her heart and was willing to take a chance on me. Stephanie has been a patient and valuable guide every step of the way and a pleasure to know.

I am grateful to Elizabeth Perle, my editor at HarperSanFrancisco, for her faith in the subject's timeliness, value, and importance and for supporting me in presenting it through my own perspective as artist and mystic. And to her gracious assistant, associate editor David Hennessy, thank you. My thanks to Terri Leonard, senior managing editor, and Priscilla Stuckey, my copyeditor, Linda Dingler, designer,

designer, Jim Warner, art director, Rebecca Fox and Calla Devlin in publicity and marketing, and everyone at Harper San Francisco whose hearts, minds, and hands went into the creation of this book.

My gratitude to Larry Dossey, June Singer, William Minor, Vern Overlee, Howard Ehrenfeld, and Lucy Malloy for valuable support, guidance, and assistance so generously given.

Visitations from the Afterlife would not have been possible without the hundreds of people from around the globe who sent me their visitation stories. So many people, near and far, generously opened their hearts and allowed me to behold their treasured secrets. My deepest gratitude goes to each. Every story is a miracle, a love letter from the Infinite, and I regret that I could not include them all. My apologies to anyone who did not hear back from me after a computer disaster that destroyed much of my correspondence and left me with no way to find you again.

I offer special gratitude to Marguerite Craig, Dorothy Adler, and Joe Adams for leaving no stone unturned in the search for stories. "I am a friend of Marguerite's," "Dorothy said I should call," and, "Joe sent me" became music to my ears.

To my spiritual family, my "root friends," whose love and support and belief in me and my work are the deep roots from which the branches, leaves, and fruit of my life emerge: your love sustains me. You mean more to me than I could ever say—Guy Robinson, Mary Atkinson, Jim Riggs, Paula Reeves, Terri Chastain, Suzanne Deats, Carol Guion, Gayle Swift, Ann Roberts, and Katie Wolfman.

With gratitude and blessings to the special friends, some old and some new, who have enriched my life beyond measure: Gail Holland, Maureen O'Toole, Shelley Marcus, Sue Prichard, Deborah Penrose, Camille Howard, Louanne LaRoche, Dixie Gamble, Frank Lawlis, Nancy Colville, Chandra Alexander, Padma Moyer, Cosmo Pagano, Ward Wieman, Monika and Malik Slosberg, Elaine Friedman, Linda and David Ragsdale, Carrell Dammann, and Richard Moyer.

Eternal thanks to my sister, Nancy Alexander, for her love and ever-constant friendship and belief in me. She is the most courageous person I know.

Thanks to my dogs, Rumi, Sophie, and Max. They are with me throughout each day, and their joy and love are woven into every page.

More than anyone on this earth, my beloved husband, Martin Dunne, has been totally supportive throughout the writing of this book. I am grateful to you for my peaceful studio and home, for teaching and reteaching me to use the word processor, for doing endless repairs of truly endless computer disasters, for providing a continual flow of morning coffee, for reading chapters again and again, and for the ten thousand other kindnesses rendered. Most of all, I thank you for your love of life, your joy, your gentleness, and your love for me.

I am ever grateful to Harry, my friend who from the other side offers me his love, friendship, and gentle guidance as he lovingly lifts my vision to the next horizon. To Harry, to Lily, and all those in the unseen who have been instrumental in the birthing and writing of this book, thank you.

So many have been a part of this effort that I could not begin to thank everyone here by name. I thank you with all of my heart.

Lee Lawson
San Luis Obispo County, California
March 17, 2000